COFFEE 4 CLOSERS

Amani "All Day" Kelly

COFFEE 4 CLOSERS

Printed in the United States of America. For information, see www.coffee4closers.com. Published by Miana Publishers, LLC.

Library of Congress cataloging-in-publication data
ISBN 978-0-9899315-0-2

TABLE OF CONTENTS

For everyone that has had a dream, no matter how big or how small, it starts with an idea, and then an action... Just do it!

~ AK

ACKNOWLEDGEMENTS

I would like to express my gratitude to the many people who saw me through this book; to all of those who provided support, talked things over, read, wrote, offered comments, allowed me to quote their remarks and assisted in the editing, proofreading and design. I had a good idea that was just an idea, until my inner circle pushed me to move forward with it.

Above all I want to thank my Daughter, my Mother, and the rest of my Family, who supported and encouraged me in spite of all the time it took me away from them. I would like to thank Jay, Norm, Lew Lew, and Phil for helping me in the process of ideation, selection, removal and editing.

Thanks to Lucyus Fevrier of Fevy Designs - without you and your expert graphic design skills, this book would never find its way to the Printer or the Web.

Last and not least: I beg forgiveness of all those who have been with me over the course of the years and whose names I have failed to mention. I will not forget you next time!

~Amani "All Day" Kelly

INTRODUCTION

Put down your coffee. Coffee's for closers.

If you work in sales, or have a pulse, then you probably know these words, or at least some version of them. They're from the flick "Glengarry Glen Ross," which is about a group of sleazy salesmen who force-feed useless plots of swampland to their sucker clients.

Now, the guys in that flick were flat-out con men, but you don't have to be a con man to appreciate the idea of coffee being for closers. In fact, the idea is very simple: you close the deal, you get to drink coffee. You don't close deals or make sales, then keep your distance from the coffee machine, 'cause you're not worthy of the prize.

In other words: Never, ever stand there relaxing like a winner when you haven't won.

This is a book by a salesperson, with collections and insight from other salespeople, and non-salespeople about who we are and what we do, and who YOU think we are. It's not an instructional guide on how to sell or negotiate, or how to get motivated to sell and negotiate; you can find plenty of that stuff elsewhere on the market. What this book does is present the *culture* of salespeople: the different types of salespeople, the different values they have, the different styles they work with, the different stories of their trade, and, of course, the different products and services they sell.

Where there are people, there are salespeople.

We're a huge part of life, and we've been around in some form or another since cavemen walked the Earth. Even way back then, you can bet there was a caveman collecting rocks, wood, and pieces of meat in exchange for letting others sit around his fire. He probably even bargained with them all, speaking only in grunts and groans.

Nowadays, of course, salespeople come in all shapes and sizes. And this book is a kind of mirror held up to the sales world, to be looked at and enjoyed by salespeople and non-salespeople alike.

This is not to say that you won't learn anything from reading this book. On the contrary, you'll probably learn a little bit more than you thought you would. And if you're new to the field of sales, you might find information here that leads you to the next level of success. It's just that the information won't be laid out in a step-by-step manner, with dull quizzes to torture you at the end of each chapter.

What you'll learn in here is how salespeople think. What makes us tick. How we function. How one communicates through psychology, and another communicates through emotion. How one makes sales by getting customers laughing, and another closes deals by creating fear. How all of us are human, even though a few of us might go out of their way to make you think otherwise!

All kidding aside, salespeople are just regular people, with our own set of codes and behaviors that are unique to our profession. For example, you'll notice that many of us have sharp little sayings that we like to repeat. One of mine goes, "If you look good, you feel good. If you feel good, you sell well." (More on that in just a little while...)

In other words, don't show up to work unshaven and with bloodshot eyes. (Even though a few of my coworkers have and still do!)

As you read and learn, you'll also chuckle, gut laugh, and even cry. Okay, well, hopefully nobody cries! This book is here to brighten your days, not make them darker. In fact, if you're a salesperson in the middle of a challenging deal, or a non-salesperson about to go buy a car, then picking up this book will give you a fast reminder that there are always others in the trenches with you, or who can relate to your own story.

Also, if you're a salesperson, you'll gain some insights into how your fellow professionals operate – and you'll likely see some version of yourself staring up at you from these pages. And if you're not a salesperson, you'll get an entertaining look at a totally unique part of life.

Salespeople are creatures of trade. They trade XYZ for $$$. Maybe XYZ is something physical, like a brand new car, or maybe it's something immaterial, like knowledge or self-confidence. Whatever it is, a good salesperson knows how to exceed expectations, and a bad one eventually runs off in search of another field.

This book tells the stories of the ones who stuck around – many of whom like to call themselves "closers." So if you're a closer, grab some coffee, and enjoy a few cups before you close this book.

(Note: After you're done reading, please stop by our website at www.coffee4closers.com to leave feedback, criticism, ridicule, and endless praise.)

PART I:
WHO ARE SALESPEOPLE?

I firmly believe that any man's finest hour, the greatest fulfillment of all that he holds dear, is that moment when he has worked his heart out in a good cause and lies exhausted on the field of battle - victorious.

~ Vince Lombardi

Common Definitions Of A Salesperson

1.) "A salesman or saleswoman"

2.) "An individual who represents and sells products and/or services for a manufacturer, wholesaler, or retailer."

One better definition of a Salesperson:

"An individual who sells goods and services to other entities. The success of a salesperson is usually measured by the amount of sales he or she is able to make during a given period, and how good that individual is in persuading others to make a purchase. If a salesperson is employed by a company, in some cases compensation can be decreased or increased based on the amount of goods or services sold."

The Salesperson's Definition of a Salesperson:

"A dynamic individual – man or woman – who with great effort goes above and beyond the call of duty to help educate and advise their clients or prospects on products or services, for which they will receive some form of bonus or commission for their hard work if a sale is made."

How The Media Portrays Salespeople
The Movies, Plays, and TV Shows Other Salespeople Will Judge You For Not Seeing... **(*BEWARE OF SPOILERS!*)**

1. DEATH OF A SALESMAN
We're going to go into this play (which has been turned into a variety of different movie adaptations) a little more later, when we examine its protagonist, Willy Loman.

For now, I'll put it to you this way:

Unless you've been living in a cave, you should know that this Arthur Miller play is the World Heavyweight Champion of American salesmen stories. In fact, whether you like this play or not, in terms of its sheer reputation as a portrait of a salesman, nothing else in our popular entertainment culture even comes close to it.

Which brings us to the matter...of its substance.

I won't lie to you: This is one dark and heavy piece of work. In fact, its very darkness might make some salespeople recoil, thinking, "WHY, oh WHY, do writers and artists have to depict us with such heaviness?"

It's a fair question, I think.

The "salesman" in American drama is generally viewed as a tragic or corrupt figure. When you walk into a show called DEATH OF A SALESMAN, you know you're not in for a cheerful lark about a winner who's setting a string of sales records!

Nope. What you get here is the decline of a once-talented door-to-door salesman, mapped out with no shortage of psychological terror and agonizing heartbreak.

4

Powerful stuff? Yes. Worth seeing? Absolutely.

But us salespeople can't help but wonder why we always get such a bad rap. The fact that the signature work that depicts us for audiences makes us look bleak, sad, and even pathetic says a lot.

Couldn't someone pound out a play called LIFE OF A SALESMAN, about a guy who's so good at selling that he retires happily to the Bahamas and spends every day aboard a yacht?

I mean, boxers got the darkness of RAGING BULL, but they also got the light of ROCKY. Lawyers may come off as sleazy sharks in most of the films they appear in, but then you have them standing tall in A FEW GOOD MEN and TO KILL A MOCKINGBIRD. Psychologists may have Hannibal Lecter to make them look like nutcases, but on the flipside they've got Robin Williams kicking butt in GOOD WILL HUNTING.

So salespeople kind of have to scrape together some positivity from the way they're depicted in popular entertainment.

I for one keep a positive attitude about this state of affairs. Maybe studying these films, plays, shows, and characters will pave the way for more uplifting content about salespeople, where we're not mocked or frowned upon or sneered at or...well, the list goes on...

For the time being, let's take a look at some more fun works, and rest assured as we go forward that NONE of them our as dark as our masterpiece, DEATH OF A SALESMAN.

2. GLENGARRY GLEN ROSS

Already, things are looking up.

Sure, GLENGARRY GLEN ROSS makes its crew of fraudster real estate salesmen look desperate, ruthless, crass, and possibly even evil...but unlike Willy Loman in DEATH OF A SALESMAN, at least this gang is actually funny.

That is, if you have David Mamet's sense of humor.

And a huge tolerance for profanity, which this play (and also exists as an amazing movie) serves up in generous portions.

Even if you don't laugh your head off at the spectacle of half a dozen real estate sharks insulting each other and ripping each other off, I'll bet my professional reputation that in any room filled with salespeople, anywhere in this country, when mention of GLENGARRY GLEN ROSS is made, people naturally start to smile.

Because this thing is a rocket of energy, giving you no end of fast talk, cutting insights, and penetrating human psychology. We'll go into a couple of these guys in detail shortly, but for now, suffice to say that every sales guy in the GLENGARRY office has his own quirks:

You've got the old veteran who's past his prime but still filled with hope and energy.

The veteran's hotshot protégé, who's so cocky he probably has posters of himself up on his bedroom wall.

The panting-desperate family man who's quick of mind but drowning in a losing streak (and thinking about robbing the office).

The dim stooge who's so mentally sluggish it's a wonder why he keeps coming back to work each day.

The by-the-book manager who comes back to work each day only because he *runs* the office, but should have been eaten by all the sharks he manages a long, long time ago.

Also, the movie version, unlike the play, has a character named BLAKE (played by Alec Baldwin) in it who's brought in to motivate the troops, but does so with such lacerating brutality that it's a miracle nobody swallows a bottle of pills right in the middle of his speech.

Are you laughing yet?

Okay: It's brutal stuff, and not for kids, but the speed, rhythm, and insight of the thing is breathtaking enough to actually make it fun.

And if its view of salespeople isn't much lighter than Arthur Miller's in DEATH OF A SALESMAN, then at least it's rescued (for the salespeople in the audience) by a less tragic attitude.

Whereas DEATH OF A SALESMAN is screaming, crying, shrieking, and sobbing with agony, GLENGARRY GLEN ROSS is kind of saying, "Look, these guys are con artists with no souls, but that's just life, baby. Get on with it."

And besides, as we all well know: Most salespeople have plenty of character, integrity, and soul.

Now there's a line to make the characters in GLENGARRY laugh...

3. WALL STREET

WALL STREET gets granted somewhat narrow inclusion on this list because it's about stock and real estate speculation, and stock trading isn't precisely "sales" in the way many people think about it.

Then again, we're putting WALL STREET high on this list because it's something of a masterpiece among American business movies. In fact, there probably hasn't been a film this quotable since the first two GODFATHERS.

Gordon Gekko (Michael Douglas) is the main character of this 1987 Oliver Stone flick – or maybe I should call him the "main event." Story-wise, the main character is Bud Fox (played by Charlie Sheen), and we follow poor Bud's descent into corruption as a result of his greed.

However, it's Gordon Gekko who keeps us watching the show.

For it's Gekko who delivers such classic lines as "Lunch is for wimps" and "Greed is good." At one point, when criticizing a competitor, he even yells, "If this guy ran a funeral parlor no one would die!"

Yeah, WALL STREET is pretty fun stuff.

Like its predecessors on this list, it's out to show the dark side of American capitalism, and how the human soul can get destroyed when a person chases the buck. In one painfully corny yet still-classic moment, Bud Fox looks out over the big city and says to himself (out loud!), "Who am I?"

It's a good question, and it turns out in the end that he's actually an okay guy. He's not cut out to run in Gekko's circle, where inside information keeps the dollars pouring in. Nah, Bud's cut from the same cloth as his dad, Carl (Martin Sheen), who believes in truth, ethics, and hard work.

Which is not to say that Bud doesn't spend most of the movie scamming people, living large, and even dating a prostitute before he arrives at his grand moral awakening (which, by the way, only happens when his dad's company gets destroyed at his own hands and his dad has a heart attack as a result!).

Anyway, here's the funny thing about WALL STREET:

Like I said, Gekko's the main attraction, and in the end, this really is Gekko's movie. The same way Hannibal Lecter walks away with THE SILENCE OF THE LAMBS even though he's not the hero (far from it, of course), Gordon Gekko not only becomes the center of attention in this film, but the film – seemingly accidentally – happens to occupy Gekko's moral universe.

To watch this movie is to get lost in a fantasy of materialism: sleek apartments and beach houses, million-dollar artwork, fast cars and limousines, suits that cost more than most people make in a month. Director Stone taps into the sheer pleasure of becoming rich, and does so at such a strong level that the movie's theme – about being a good, decent, hardworking, creative person and not living off the buying and selling of others – kind of doesn't register the way it should.

So let's set the record straight for just a moment: Bud Fox, good guy. Gordon Gekko, bad guy. Salespeople should never lie, cheat, or steal. As Bud's mentor in his office tells him, "There are no short cuts."

Oliver Stone got dismayed over the years as he realized people thought Gekko was a hero. Stock brokers would approach him and Michael Douglas on the street and say they wanted to work on Wall Street after seeing the movie. This strange turn of events haunted the director and actor's souls, so years later they teamed up again for WALL STREET: MONEY NEVER SLEEPS, an oddball sequel where Gekko works on becoming a good person.

The problem is, a guy like that has no soul, and truth be told, anyone who would idolize such a character needs to do what Bud Fox does, and eventually look in the mirror.

As for those who *didn't* look in the mirror, check out...

4. BOILER ROOM

The stock traders in BOILER ROOM watch WALL STREET to get motivated. They hang out eating pizza and quoting every line from the movie as it runs on one of their big-screen television sets.

Just like GLENGARRY GLEN ROSS owes a spiritual debt to DEATH OF A SALESMAN, BOILER ROOM would not exist without WALL STREET. It's

WALL STREET for the telemarketing class. Accordingly, it features a group of guys (many of whom look like kids) selling junk stock from a fluorescent-lit trading room located *far* away from the actual Wall Street. They bark into telephones, promising clients the world, and delivering absolutely nothing upon closing.

Seth Davis (Giovanni Ribisi) starts the movie off in a bind: He's making good money running an illegal casino, but his dad, who works as a judge (!), is ready to strangle him if he doesn't go and do something legitimate. One night, a couple of Seth's pals show up to gamble at his place, and he can't help but be impressed with the fancy car one of them drives.

He wants to know where they're getting the cash from.

And soon he learns about the stock trading gig.

The tragedy is, Seth is told that it's a legit operation. But over at J.T. Marlin, the bumb firm where he ends up getting a job, only the highest guys on the totem pole know the clients are getting ripped off. The illusion of legitimacy is kept well intact for the junior brokers.

And day in and day out, they pick up their phones and rip off people's life savings.

It's heartbreaking to watch this thing unfold, knowing how eager Seth is to impress his establishment father, then seeing his hopes of becoming a millionaire shatter as he pieces together the fact that his employers are criminals.

Eventually, Seth cooperates with the F.B.I. and helps them orchestrate a raid on the place. By the time the flick ends, he's right back where he started: Looking for a job.

Okay, time out:

I admit that this chapter offers a grim analysis. You bought a book about salespeople and now find yourself reading about scammers, hustlers, and forces of evil. But the cool thing about BOILER ROOM is, even though it's not as visionary or dramatic as WALL STREET, it arrives at its moral point in a more convincing manner.

The fellas at J.T. Marlin never once look cool or enviable here. They're made out to be second-rate phonies from the start. In fact, as I said, they're child-like, and often come off as teenagers stuffed into grown men's suits. When we see one of their houses, it's not even decorated; it's like the poor kid didn't know he could actually pick out furniture to put in there. When the J.T. boys go out to a bar for a drink, they get made fun of by the legitimate stock traders for being a small-time, laughable gang.

Sure, the guys in BOILER ROOM sling all the quick, funny, witty banter that's a staple of the salesperson genre, but when you see them ripping off their clients, you feel uncomfortable; it gets under your skin.

The blind spot in WALL STREET is, you never see the result of the scams and victimization, aside from what they do to one of the victimizers' souls. In BOILER ROOM, you're put into scene-by-scene awareness that what's going on is wrong. There's no charismatic

Gordon Gekko to mount a hypnotic counter-argument.

You're told, flat-out, exactly what Martin Sheen in WALL STREET stands for: *Do something real for a living or you're a loser.*

5. JERRY MAGUIRE

Already, I sense you sensing a change in tone.

JERRY MAGUIRE is no doubt a brighter, funnier, and more optimistic piece of work than the four we just spent time discussing. Like WALL STREET and BOILER ROOM, it shows us a side of the sales world that doesn't immediately square with our most prominent thoughts about sales:

It's all about the fast-paced world of sports agents.

And it would *just about* make it as the TO KILL A MOCKINGBIRD of salesperson flicks, but it can't quite claim that title because (a) agents do an unconventional form of selling, and can't comfortably represent *all* salespeople the way Willy Loman can and (b) Jerry Maguire, played by Tom Cruise, though noble, impassioned, excellent at his job, and even pretty inspiring, is a little bit silly – and spends most of the movie getting depicting as a loser.

In fact, filmmaker Cameron Crowe is on the record saying he wanted to give audiences a change in how they get served Tom Cruise, for up until JERRY MAGUIRE, he was always a winner – cocky, smiling, all-too-sure of himself – but this time out he's kind of a lovable embarrassment.

But just because JERRY MAGUIRE isn't quite the most inspirational sales movie of all-time doesn't mean it's not a great movie, and doesn't mean salespeople shouldn't claim it and its values as their own.

Interestingly, when this movie starts, Maguire hasn't done anything illegal or even particularly immoral, but he's having an existential crisis because he hates his place in the world. In other words, he's sick to his core because he feels like he's not doing anything of value. One night, seized by passion, he types up a mission statement for his industry, stating in no uncertain terms that theirs should be a business of heart, soul, and integrity.

He passes the mission statement out to his coworkers. He gets applauded for his efforts. He's 34 years old and feeling like he's finally arrived in life.

And then he's taken to lunch and fired.

The problem? He spoke out against the bottom line. That's a huge no-no among agents and – let's face it – salespeople in general.

When Maguire's clearing out his office, he goes into a mad scramble, calling all his clients and trying to persuade them to stick with him even though he's leaving the firm. When the smoke clears, the only one who sticks with him is Rod Tidwell (Cuba Gooding, Jr.), a football player who's agonizing because he hasn't broken out yet and the big paydays keep eluding him.

Maguire and Tidwell – whether they like it or not – are a perfect match, for they're both overloaded with potential yet haven't managed to seize the big-time. For much of the movie, amidst story lines involving their respective love lives, the two go around wondering if the other will eventually prove to be a worthy investment.

Now, this movie is famous for a single line: "Show Me The Money!"

That's a great line, and there's nothing wrong with it. Tidwell forces Maguire to scream those very words back to him before he agrees to stay onboard as his client. There's a vivid value there, namely that money talks and...all the rest...walks.

But "Show Me The Money" – even though audiences still recite those words to this day – isn't exactly what JERRY MAGUIRE is about.

At a key moment later in the film, while Tidwell complains to Maguire about his lack of career momentum, Maguire points out to Tidwell that in his marriage, he's all *heart*, and as a result, his marriage is great. Maguire then says that if Tidwell brought the kind of heart to the field that he brings to his marriage, his game would surely improve.

In other words, it's back to the Maguire mission statement: Don't play for bucks, play for heart.

As it turns out, Maguire himself has to learn this very lesson, for despite the heart he gives to his work as an agent, he's not giving enough heart to his own marriage.

JERRY MAGUIRE is the story of these two men gaining values from each other, and boosting each other's life performances as a result.

Nobody does anything illegal. Nobody's soul gets destroyed. And although the theme of heart outweighing dollars might annoy some people, I have to go ahead and say that it holds water:

For the best salespeople I know are the ones who approach the game with their hearts invested.

I hope you've enjoyed the little detour. Now let's return to our previously scheduled moral outrage...

6. THANK YOU FOR SMOKING

Right away, from that title, you know we're back in darker territory.

THANK YOU FOR SMOKING revolves around Nick Naylor (Aaron Eckhart), who brings to our discussion yet another form of sales that isn't commonly thought of:

Lobbying.

Naylor's job is to lobby on behalf of smoking. He works for a tobacco-company-funded lobby that is perpetually "researching" whether or not there's a hard link between smoking and lung cancer. Naturally, the movie's got one foot planted squarely in unreality, though the clever part is that such a lobby – and lobbyist – could very easily exist.

The film's plot isn't its most memorable aspect, but the character of Nick Naylor more than makes up for it. Not only is he a fast thinker and a smooth talker, but he maintains an active interest in the art of debate. As far as he's concerned, everything under the sun is open to debate, and if his job's got him occupying a particular position, then that's just the way it is. He simply has to do his best to get that position across for the sake of his company.

What's interesting about this flick is how it adds to the moral layers of the ones above by showing us a guy who's not particularly bad or evil, doing something perfectly legal, yet hurting millions of people in the process. THANK YOU FOR SMOKING puts us in touch with the fact that many legitimate activities have dark undertones, yet we don't look at these activities as negative because we're programmed to accept the status quo.

This is good territory for salespeople to travel as they mature and advance in their professions, because it's easy to get so caught up in the act of selling that you get numb about the thing being sold.

But what's being sold is where the real value is, and if you're applying your sales skill to moving questionable goods, then something's out of whack. Take the good part of the equation (you) and leave the bad part (the garbage product) behind.

7. MAD MEN

Back in the 1950s, guys who sold advertising on Madison Avenue got into the habit of calling themselves "mad men." On the one hand, they were "ad men," but in the meantime they were on "Mad..." Avenue, so the nickname stuck.

And naturally, the implication is also that on

some level...they were insane.

Don Draper runs the ad agency in the TV series MAD MEN. Only "Don Draper" isn't his real name; he used to be called Dick Whitman. While fighting in the Korean War, Whitman saw his superior, Don Draper, killed in front of him. Knowing that Draper was soon headed back to the states, Whitman switched identities with the dead man and got to leave the theater of war.

In the process, he gained some distance from his actual family in the U.S., and started a whole new life.

And I haven't even mentioned the amount of nicotine, alcohol, and "romance" this man consumes.

The rest of the cast isn't much of a picnic, either. The show casts its eye on the addictions, intolerance, and adultery of its historical time period, depicting its slate of "ad men" as lying, cheating, egotistical, amoral menaces.

In fact, if you're a salesperson looking for inspiration and validation, then MAD MEN is *not* the place to start!

Key Fictional Sales People In American Drama And Comedy

You read the above heading correctly.

We're going to be talking about MEN in this section. I put the word in caps not because I'm about to go into some masculine, moose-hunting frenzy, but because it is the icon of the salesMAN who has dominated in our culture's popular storytelling.

The good news is, somehow I don't think my women readers will mind very much once they read about and/or recall the characters on this list. On the contrary, they'll probably breathe a sigh of relief to have not been placed in such questionable company...

That said, even though we're about to look at a collection of hustlers, sleazes, and outright sharks, every single one of the six characters looked at in this chapter has tangible redeeming qualities. Accordingly, we're going to take the bad with the good, and dig in to find out what these fellas can teach us about the profession of sales.

Then maybe someday a list like this will have some more inspiring characters on it, and be a prouder place for women to appear.

WILLY LOMAN

Willy's the key, the cream of the crop.

This doesn't mean he's the finest salesman on this list – though in his prime, he may arguably have been just that. What it does mean is that Willy Loman is the most famous and iconic salesman in American storytelling. Nobody else even comes near him. When Arthur Miller wrote DEATH OF A SALESMAN back in the late 1940s, he created an enduring masterpiece about the very soul of a salesman.

And needless to say, the play is a pretty dark piece of work.

Simply stated (and forgive me if I'm not communicating on the level of a first-rate drama critic), Willy's losing his mind in the play. A traveling salesman who once ruled his field by way of Grade-A knowledge and unbeatable people skills, Willy's getting old, and his head is getting soft.

When we meet him, in fact, he's half living in a fantasy world. He's remembering the good old days, back when life was filled with promise and the (real) world seemed like it was his for the taking. Back then, he was a beast of positivity and ambition.

Nowadays, he's literally dying right before our eyes. Job is fading, relationships are fading, mind is fading.

For those of you who are still reading and haven't yet cried yourselves to sleep, I can state with confidence that there is indeed an *inspiring* message to be taken from DEATH OF A SALESMAN. Sure, drama snobs will roll their eyes at this notion, insisting that the play is a wholly persuasive look at how capitalism corrupts and drains the human soul, but if you'll allow me, I'd like to throw in some alternative ideas.

Why Willy Loman Rocks

Willy Loman rocks because, plain and simple, at one point in time, he was one of the best door-to-door salesmen around. Sure, the play has to view him through a dark lens, because otherwise there would be no conflict and therefore no drama, but in his prime, he was a model of excellence.

He talked the talk.

He walked the walk.

He built good relationships and knew how to get close with his customers. He was a fine role model for his two sons, Biff and Harold (aka Happy). He showed up to his marriage with energy and an infectious enthusiasm for life.

Looking at it this way, the only sad thing about Willy Loman is that eventually – yes – he dies!

So does everyone!

But it's not really a wise idea for salesmen to dwell on that. You know who else shouldn't dwell on it? People in general! So what? The guy declined one day and lost his mind. It could happen to anyone.

If you want to call my man Willy a "has been," go ahead, but at least he avoided being a "never was."

And if you want the truth, I don't even think Willy was a "has been" in the strictest sense of the term. Sure, his best days passed him by, but let's be sober about something:

Sales is a game of numbers.

Your volume of sales determines your value in whatever context you work in. Sure, you can have good relationships with the customers, but if you're not selling then, well, they're not really customers anymore, are they?

And since sales boils down to numbers, all salespeople have a peak period.

It's mathematical law. In sales, you have a point where you're at your best. Whereas a great actor may have several performances spread over the years that rank high, and a great lawyer may win several tough cases throughout his or her career, a great salesperson will have a single period or sale or group of sales that represents a record figure. It's inevitable.

So Willy Loman had his day in the sun. He was a winner; the real thing; that's why his eventual downfall is worthy of a tragic treatment.

There can't be dark without light. And Willy Loman once stirred up a lot of light, even if DEATH OF A SALESMAN doesn't focus on it.

SHELLY "THE MACHINE" LEVENE

Here's another piece of work for ya.

Shelly "The Machine" Levene, like Willy Loman, is past his prime. But he's still got his wits about him, and he's still wholly capable of pulling off a dazzling sale.

The problem is, his personality's a disaster. If this guy existed in real life, he would suck all the air clean out of the room. Phony laughter. Plastic smiles. Forced pats on the back.

With the play GLEGARRY GLEN ROSS, David Mamet was throwing his hat in the ring with Arthur Miller and DEATH OF A SALESMAN. And you know what? He came damn close to tying with Miller's "Greatest Salesman Play of All-Time," for GLENGARRY is an incredible piece of work.

The key difference between the two plays may be that Mamet's salesmen characters have less heart than Willy Loman does (even if Mamet has a more comedic attitude than Miller).

(*SPOILER ALERT!*)

Shelly Levene's so corrupt that he teams up with another sales guy at his sham real estate office and robs the premium leads from the manager's office. Can you believe this sleaze ball? And when he's caught red-handed, he starts to talk and stammer and chatter and swindle to try to "sell" his way out of trouble.

But that's not a sale that poor Shelley can close, 'cause in the end it's clear he's headed to jail.

Shame, too. Because on the very morning after the robbery, Levene actually manages to close a good deal in a legit fashion (even though his manager later says the clients are full of it). So in addition to being a thief, Levene's a pathetic thief, 'cause he didn't even have to steal in the first place!

If only he had held out for one more day.

Why Shelley Rocks

I'm sure you feel like taking a shower after

reading about this con artist, but Shelly "The Machine" Levene didn't earn his nickname for nothing.

For one thing, the guy – courtesy of David Mamet – is such a master of velvety-confident speech that he could probably talk a toddler out of his breakfast cereal.

For another thing, the big SPOILER above comes as a big surprise at the end of GLENGARRY, for Shelly's so smooth that we've spent the whole play suspecting *other* characters robbed the office.

So at least give the guy points for maintaining a credible surface.

Levene may be desperate, over-the-hill, and morally compromised, but there's still enough fuel in his engine to keep his quick mind moving and his quick tongue talking.

And that, my friends, is worth paying some attention to.

RICKY ROMA

Ricky Roma works in the same office as Shelly "The Machine" Levene. In fact, on the face of it, Roma seems like a guiltier soul than Levene (even though that point can be argued, particularly since Levene – the older of the two men – is Roma's mentor).

I have a sneaking suspicion that it was Roma who gave The Machine his nickname. He loves to say "The Machine" with relish, celebrating the older, more seasoned salesman.

But it's hard to watch him do so without your B.S.

alarm going off.

Because let's face it: Ricky Roma is as dishonest, corrupt, greedy, and selfish as any salesman in history – imaginary or otherwise.

I mean, this guy actually spends most of the play closing a deal by manipulating a lead's (apparent) latent homosexuality. Roma acts very subtly gay, playing with his hair and touching the lead's arm, to create the illusion of a close bond between them and seize the poor guy's money.

And I can't think of any tactic lower than that type of manipulation.

Shelly Levene may be a scoundrel, but Roma brings sales work to the level of prostitution. He sits in a Chinese restaurant with his target – um, lead – for hours, talking on and on and pretending they're becoming best friends – and possibly more than that.

All just to put money in his own pocket.

By the time GLENGARRY GLEN ROSS is over, about the only good thing to say about Ricky Roma is "Well, at least he didn't rob the place!"

Why Ricky Roma Rocks

This is a tough one, because short of his amazing gifts of speech and persuasion, Roma is a pretty dark soul.

But let's give him props for something important:

He's the top guy on the boards. And he's ENJOYING it.

That's the key to Roma's presence in

GLENGARRY. There's a big sales board in the center of the office, and Roma's maintaining a comfortable lead over his coworkers. He's a fighter, a survivor, a resourceful thinker, and a guy who knows how to keep a winning streak alive.

Every salesperson can benefit from Roma's example in this regard.

In sales, you're not always up. So when you're up, be like Roma and get excited, let it fuel you, use your confidence in the way you talk and move, and maintain the momentum before the next (inevitable) downturn.

No one does winning quite like Ricky Roma.

LARRY DALLAS

The name sounds familiar, doesn't it?

If you're having trouble placing it, it's because it belongs to a character who was made out to be such scum that you'd probably rather forget him.

Larry Dallas lived in the apartment above Jack Tripper's (John Ritter) in the 70s and 80s television sitcom THREE'S COMPANY.

It's important to include him on our list because he represents a universal American symbol of salesmen:

The used car salesman.

There are plenty of used car salesmen in movies, plays, books, and TV shows, but what makes Larry so compelling is the SHAME he feels over his job.

When women ask him what he does for a living, he'll give ANY answer but the real one.

For Larry knows – like all of us do – that "used car salesman" is synonymous with "sleaze." Like any stereotype, this is mean-spirited stuff, but the grain of truth that upholds it stems from the fact that used car salesmen sell a product that's already aged and worn, and are therefore in a prime position to lie about the product's value.

Moreover, and more simply, they sell something that's generally understood to be second-rate, and that puts them in a unique position.

For nobody's out there selling used food. Nobody sells used medical equipment. Used paint? Used newspapers?

Don't make me laugh.

If it's not new, it's seen as less valuable. Now, granted, we all buy plenty of stuff – homes, books, appliances, clothes – that isn't brand new, but only the car industry keeps that key word, "used", attached to its products.

Maybe because on some level, they're shrugging and saying, "Look, guys, we know how second-rate our products are."

Or at least Larry Dallas seems to feel that way.

Why Larry Rocks

Wait! Scratch that.

Larry doesn't rock. Jeez, remember that guy? He was a charmless, vapid, egomaniacal womanizer who probably had various chemical addictions that the network wouldn't allow to be examined on the air.

I'm not throwing Larry to the curb because he sold used cars.

I'm throwing him to the curb because in addition to being a grind, he was *ashamed* of being a salesman.

And no salesperson (except for a criminal) should ever be ashamed of what they do.

AL BUNDY

I can almost hear the studio audience cheering.

Al Bundy was another sitcom salesman, like Larry Dallas, but unlike Larry, Al was open about what he did.

Open about it...and miserable about it.

For Al Bundy sold women's shoes.

And to hear him talk about it, it sounded like his only customers were overweight old women with nasty personalities.

With Al's luck, maybe they were.

The main character of MARRIED WITH CHILDREN rose to such high prominence in our national collective consciousness because with Al Bundy, there were no secrets. The guy wasn't cunning or sleazy enough to be anyone but himself. In fact, I'd go as far as to say that Al Bundy wasn't sleazy at all.

Disgusting? Yes. Depressing? Sure. Angry? Of course. Deluded? Yep. Stupid? Certainly.

But he had a conscience, and a soul, and on that show's 11 seasons, he never accumulated the reputation of a criminal salesman. This isn't GLENGARRY GLEN

ROSS we're talking about; Al Bundy punched in his time clock, sold the shoes, and slumped home to his miserable life.

And in doing so, he bore a certain admirable nobility.

Why Al Bundy Rocks

This section alone could fill a whole book.

Al Bundy rocks because he's loyal to his wife even though she drives him crazy. Al Bundy rocks because he loves his kids even though they reflect back to him the worst of himself. Al Bundy rocks because he somehow manages to keep the mortgage paid despite working as a shoe salesman (or maybe he was always behind on his payments; who knows?).

And I haven't even gotten to Al Bundy's value as a salesman.

What can salespeople learn from this famous Illinois shoe salesman?

It's not a sexy word, but it's still a valuable one: *Steadiness.*

He wasn't choppy in his life trajectory. The guy sold shoes. Did he like it? No. Did he feel demeaned by it? Yes. But he stuck with it, because that's what was available to him, and he showed up and preserved a stable life, keeping his family clothed, housed, and fed in the process.

That is, if you could call Peg Bundy's wardrobe actual "clothing."

DEL GRIFFITH

In a way, we've saved the best for last here – or at least saved the nicest for last.

'Cause Del Griffith, the shower curtain ring salesman played by John Candy in PLANES, TRAINS, AND AUTOMOBILES isn't exactly a bad guy. Okay, yeah, he steals the credit card of his traveling companion, Neal Page (Steve Martin). And he kind of screws over some customers by selling them shower curtain rings and pretending they're fine jewels. And he talks way too much, and has nauseating personal hygiene.

But somehow, despite all that, the guy has an enormous heart.

After all, even though he steals the credit card, he does so on a whim, and truly intends to give it back. And the customers who wear his shower curtain rings as earrings are actually thrilled about their purchases. And he might talk nonstop, but it's because he wants to be friendly and well-liked.

As for his hygiene, well – okay – there's really no excuse for that.

PLANES, TRAINS, AND AUTOMOBILES has had a gradual ascent to classic status. After John Candy passed away, when people looked back at his body of work, they began to isolate his role in this film as one of his best (or his outright best). It also came to be regarded as the best film he was ever involved in. A classic American road story about a sales guy (Candy) and a marketing guy (Martin) en route home to spend

Thanksgiving with their families, it's got so many elements of greatness: the timeless humor, the open plains, the holiday appeal, the family theme, and of course two legendary comedians at its center.

But key for our purposes is the presence of a salesman.

Like with DEATH OF A SALESMAN, this movie knows that there's something about salesmen that is uniquely American. They're part of our country's soul. We thrive on free trade, and the salesman – salesperson – is the purest agent of that trade.

Del Griffith is a guy whom many of us have met in real life. Like he says, "What you see is what you get." He's unpretentious, big-hearted, out for a good time, and as sensitive as a young kid.

To not love this guy is to have a heart of stone.

Why Del Griffith Rocks

Jeez, do I still have more to say?

You bet I do. I haven't yet analyzed Griffith as an actual salesman. And when I do, you'll see that he teaches us a good deal.

The key moment when we see Del Griffith's talent for sales is when he and Page are low on funds, and he springs into action, selling off shower curtain rings to strangers for cash. Sure, he claims they're of immense value and can be worn as jewelry, but let's put aside the fraudulent (and clearly immoral) aspect of his sales campaign.

What's important for us to pay attention to is that

the guy is quick on his feet.

All the best salespeople in the world have this trait. They improvise. They know how to talk. They know how to get people conversing and smiling and laughing. They have the guts to approach strangers and turn them into clients – and even turn them into friends.

Del Griffith not only knows how to unload some stock when he's in a tight corner, but he's also undeniably great *with the people*. Note the moment when he and Page are on a crowded bus, and all the passengers take turns singing classic American songs. When Neal Page is pressed to start a new song, he hits them with a number that nobody knows, and everybody looks at him like he's an alien.

Saving the day, Griffith dives in with the theme song to "The Flintstones."

Next thing you know, everybody's singing their hearts out.

This is a key insight into Del Griffith's greatness, and his value as a salesman. He knows what regular people are into. He knows what they'll like and what will make them respond. Like I said before, this guy is not only far from pretentious, but he probably only half knows the meaning of that word.

This lesson is a terrific one for all salespeople.

You have to be into people. Get to know them. Embrace the side of you that loves them. An enemy to society will never succeed in sales. If that's your thing, go and be a graffiti artist or something. If you want to sell, you have to be tuned into people's drives, desires, interests, and fascinations.

And it helps if – like Del Griffith – you have a desire to be giving, too.

Because in the end, the best form of selling is giving. You want your clients to be better off after knowing you than they were before you came along. Whatever you placed into their lives should make those lives richer, fuller, deeper, more satisfying, and/or easier.

Del Griffith may have only sold shower curtain rings, but hey, I doubt any of his customers' shower curtains ever fell down.

And as for the ones who wore them as earrings, they actually didn't look half bad!

Famous Sales People

MARY KAY ASH

This entrepreneurial giant from Texas founded Mary Kay Cosmetics, a Multi-level Marketing company with so much power that rumor has it they can override Congressional decisions made in Washington. Okay, fine, they're not THAT powerful, but what this woman has achieved is pretty extreme. She started off with more of a visionary cause than an intention to launch a business. What happened was, she worked for a company where she trained a fellow employee how to do his job. This man received a promotion instead of Mary Kay, even though she had taught him everything. Outraged, she retired. She planned to write a book to inspire women how to succeed in business. But a funny thing happened on the way to the publisher – the book mutated into a business plan, and within its pages was Mary Kay's ideal business. She became determined to start her cosmetics line. She did so with her husband, but he died of a heart attack right at the beginning, so her sons stepped in to help in his absence. What started as a modest enterprise in a little storefront morphed into a monolithic industry giant.

DALE CARNEGIE

If you haven't read Dale Carnegie's famous book HOW TO WIN FRIENDS AND INFLUENCE PEOPLE, then that should be the first sales book on your list. In fact, put this thing aside until you're finished with that one. I'm as competitive a salesman as any other, but not when it comes to Carnegie. He started his career as a salesman, but yearned to be more of a performer. So he tried his hand at acting, but when that didn't work out, he gave lecturing a shot. Shortly after starting, he discovered a terrific way to make people overcome their fear of public speaking: By talking about something that made them angry. He asked his students to express anger, and they went on and on, no matter who was listening. As Carnegie heard his students' words, he discovered a vivid streak in American people's character where they desire confidence. Still a salesman at heart, he began to write books designed to boost people's confidence levels, and the resulting body of work, in terms of books, lectures, and courses, has become legendary.

BILLY MAYS

Billy Mays' path to success teaches us all an important lesson: Just because someone's your rival, doesn't mean they have to be your enemy. With this wisdom in tow, Mays became friends with Max Appel, a competitor of his in the sales world. Appel ran Orange Glo International, which sold cleaning products including Kaboom, Orange Glo, OxiClean, and Orange Clean. Appel put Mays on the Home Shopping Network to sell his goods, and the sales went through the roof. Billy Mays became famous for his epic, incredible energy. Not a big fan of subtlety, he sold with force, vitality, and a loud, commanding voice. Too grand for this world, he died too young, at 50. But the imprint he made on salespeople culture will never be forgotten.

ZIG ZIGLAR

Zig Ziglar was an author and salesman, yet his influence as a motivational speaker was most widely felt. This is the guy who said, "What you get by achieving your goals is not as important as what you become by achieving your goals." He also graced us with the words, "If you go looking for a friend, you're going to find they're very scarce. If you go out to be a friend, you'll find them everywhere." He was a grand human being with a limitless insight into how to live life as an effective and contented person. You want one more quote? I know I do. Here you go: "Outstanding people have one thing in common: an absolute sense of mission." Man, there's no messing with Zig Ziglar. He was in a class by himself.

LARRY ELLISON

Larry Ellison's no slouch in the quotes department either. It was he who said, "Great achievers are driven, not so much by the pursuit of success, but by the fear of failure." Now, who exactly is this guy? Well, if you look at his business card, you'll see the words "Founder: Oracle Corporation" on it. And to hear him describe it, he didn't ascend in life by being a driven, single-minded cutthroat. No, Larry's initial goal was to simply create an environment where he enjoyed working. Now – untold fortunes later – I get the feeling he's REALLY enjoying himself! Techno-genius, visionary, and bottomless fount of information, I get the strange feeling that Mr. Ellison has somehow figured out a way to live in the future.

How "Regular" People See Salespeople

Well, perhaps using the word "regular" in the heading above isn't entirely fair, as I maintain the concrete opinion that salespeople are regular people, just like anyone else. However, the fact remains that some people are salespeople and others aren't (mind-blowing revelation, huh?!). And as long as this distinction exists, those who aren't in the sales realm will continue to form opinions of those who are.

Following is a compilation of quotes from non-salespeople about salespeople, compiled by way of extensive research, study, and personal experience. Along with each quote, I will provide some commentary to offer an alternative (i.e., salesman's) point-of-view.

Ed from Florida Says:

"I don't care for salespeople. They're too pushy. And all they care about is being persuasive. In fact, let's be honest here: They'll do ANYTHING to close a sale! All they care about is themselves, and maybe their families."

Whoa! Ed, buddy! Where do I even begin? What are you doing, overdosing on stereotypical thinking over there? How about a little bit of NUANCE and DIVERSITY in your thought process? We are NOT all pushy, persuasion-obsessed, relentless, and self-absorbed, all right? And if you're not convinced, well, I'm confident I can SELL you on my position. You can easily be persuaded...Oh, wait. Oops.

Vivan from Pittsburgh Says:

"Oh, salespeople? They're all just a bunch of fast talkers."

Vivian, let me tell you about an ex-colleague of mine. We'll call him Ned. I can assure you that Ned talked so slow that he could make a tortoise furious with impatience. The guy's metabolism was so relaxed that I'm pretty sure he was legally dead. So don't go calling all of us fast-talkers! Some of us are as dull and sluggish as drying paint!

Sulai From Atlanta says:

"Salespeople are persistent and smooth with words."

Now hold on just one second, Sulai! We are not-- oh, hold on. That's not so bad. Never mind. YES! Yes, we are persistent and smooth with words. Finally, a little respect!

Jen From Beverly Hills Says:

"The people in your profession are all just pleasers."

Hmm, now we're into some tricky territory. "Pleasers" are certainly a very specific type. Outside of the business world, being a pleaser tends to be a negative thing. The conventional wisdom goes as follows: If you're always out to please people, they'll step all over you, and even if they don't, you'll get burned out because you're always putting others ahead of yourself. However, in the sales world, aiming to please isn't necessarily a bad thing. After all, "the customer is always right," right? A good salesperson should aim to please. If the customer begins to take unfair advantage – becoming a greedy vampire in search of MORE – then it's time to draw the line. But until that instance, I'll go ahead and accept the "pleasers" term as a not-so-bad one.

Vinnie From New York Says:
"Salesmen are inherently dishonest 'cause they're so desperate!"

Okay, I'm in no rush to argue with a guy named Vinnie who lives in New York City, but maybe – just maybe – calling us dishonest simply means that you're not a very trusting soul. Do salespeople experience desperation at times? Sure, if sales are slow or a given gig's not panning out, desperation might creep into the picture. But desperation is a variable, not a constant. So to go ahead and assume we're all lying out of desperation only hurts YOU, the customer, in the end. Go ahead and try starting from a place of trust and receptiveness, and THEN if a red flag arises, you'll be able to spot it with a clear mind.

Taylor From San Francisco Says:
"You know what I've found? Salespeople tend to be very insightful."

Hey! Now we're talking! It doesn't have to be abuse all day long, I suppose. And I'll tell you what: I happen to agree with this one (no surprise there, right?). I think that a quality salesperson tends to have one very powerful tool in his or her arsenal: intuition. We're able to read between the lines. This ability aids us in picking up on what others are thinking, feeling, planning, fearing, and so on. Good salespeople generally have the ability to anticipate what their customers are going to say, and without intuition – or what Taylor terms "insight" – we wouldn't be able to do so. So cheers to Taylor for not only being positive, but for hitting on a key concept!

However, TAYLOR also goes on to say: "You fellas are also pretty competitive."

Ahem, wonderful. You couldn't stop at something sunny and uncontroversial, could you, Taylor? First off, we're not all "fellas," which should be perfectly clear in this day and age. Now, more critically, the word "competitive" belongs in a similar category as "pleaser." In most walks of life – particularly outside of business and sports and/or other games – being competitive is not the most charming quality. If you're too competitive with your friends and relatives, you're pretty likely to look around and see that they've abandoned you. However, in business and the other places I mentioned, a competitive spirit isn't necessarily a negative. We measure our success in sales by way of numbers. Usually, salespeople grouped together in one setting are all aware of what each other are earning. Be that as it may, why is it so unethical to look at the board and think, "Heck, I'd like to be doing better than Josh?" It's human nature, and it thrives within the sales world. So I reject the negative connotation of the word "competitive" when it comes to salespeople, unless we're down at the bar telling the bartender we can pour tastier shots. Then we're just big jerks.

Kris Dawn From Brooklyn says:

"Sales is just a job that people go into when they're not educated to do something better."

Jeez. Thanks, Kris Dawn. Way to get right to the point, and take all the air out of the room. Well, allow me to be as diplomatic as possible in the face of what is probably the cruelest and most demeaning thing that others say about salespeople:

Sure, we don't have to train for years and years like doctors or lawyers. And sure, we don't have any special titles before our names, like "President" or "Colonel."

And speaking of colonels, I'll admit that our lives aren't on the line, but our jobs certainly could be if we are not hitting our sales targets.

But you know what? Human beings are creatures of commerce. We buy and sell things all day long. We think about money all day long. We're *always* about to buy something. And be that as it may, salespeople might just be the most NATURAL professionals in the world.

We're natives to the human race. We've always been here, and until robots take over all the jobs, we'll probably always remain here. And not only are we a critical and foundational aspect of human existence, but let me state something equally true and even more profound:

Not Everybody Can Do What We Do.

There, I said it. Somebody had to! We're usually too polite to state this out in public, but it takes a sharp mind and expert communication skills to sell. Now, let me ask you: Is every doctor or lawyer you've met possessed of a sharp mind and communication expertise?

Of course not. So there!

I rest my case. Thank you, Your Honor (aka Kris Dawn from the Brooklyn).

Rex From Vermont Says:

"Are salespeople even still around? I thought all that stuff has gone to the Internet."

Whoa! Just when I thought I couldn't get any more disheartened, Rex goes ahead and makes a statement about the extinction of my profession.

Nope, sorry, Rex. Bookstores are closing, music stores are closing, lots of people are shopping online, but the salesperson is as active as ever. In fact, I'm going to go ahead and say that the Information Age has made us leaner and shrewder than ever, to the point where we're so effective in presenting our goods or services that it's harder to flag us as salespeople.

Think about it. The last time you bought a phone, you probably didn't even realize how deeply and effectively the sales rep was operating on you. In fact, the key word there is "rep"; to you, they just seemed like somebody who worked at the store.

But that was indeed a salesperson.

Many times, the role of the salesperson is mixed with something else. A bartender's there to serve drinks, but tune in closely to his or her words, and you're likely to find some selling going on. The same goes for the hotel manager who says to you, "Leaving so soon, Mr. Jameson? We'll hope to see you again."

See that guy working on you? Making you feel like "part of the family"? He's probably being sincere, but he's also planting the seed of a very real sale.

So in summary: We haven't gone away. If anything, we're blending in now more than ever.

Stephanie From Toronto Says:
"I think salespeople are awesome. I mean, they make the best characters, and they talk in more colorful ways than other professionals."

Ah, now we're talking (no pun intended)! Stephanie and I happen to have a great deal in common. I wish I knew what she did for a living, 'cause I'm kind of praying she's not "one of us." I mean, sorry to sound down on myself, but we don't usually catch this kind of praise from outsiders.

But you know what? Stephanie's 100 percent right! This book wouldn't even work were Stephanie's wisdom not profound. We've got a ton of soul, color, talk, and personality. There should be parades in our honor. And even if the general public didn't show up, it wouldn't matter:

It'd be a good morale booster.

'Cause salespeople rock, and we need to reinforce that fact.

And last but hardly least, PAM FROM AUSTIN says: "I can describe salespeople in a single word: coin-operated."

First of all, I could make the argument that that's TWO words, but I see the dash, and I don't have time to get into that right now. More importantly, I get what you're saying: That we're ruled by money. Doesn't matter what we're selling, huh? If it makes money then we just want to plug right into it, don't we? Well, in many cases money is indeed a salesperson's leading motive, but no matter who the salesperson is and what they're selling, they're not going to succeed unless they operate with SUBSTANCE. It's one thing to be stationed in a stark telemarketing office, calling people to sell off information that can be found for free on the web – and never even bothering to read or even see the product to begin with. That never lasts. It's another thing, however, to sell Real Estate and know every detail of the properties you're showing in your bones and nerve endings. That kind of rigor goes beyond a simple appetite for the buck. So if you think salespeople are "coin-operated" machines, then I'll go ahead and agree with you.

And I'll only add that just the *bad ones* fit that description.

In Summary: How "YOU" Envision "US"

It's clear that non-salespeople can perceive salespeople with an assortment of negative stereotypes. Though I'm not about to declare that there's some grand witch hunt going on against salespeople, I will say that we're generally perceived as being greedy, manipulative, dishonest, and many other less-than-delightful things. Underlying these stereotypes is an even uglier perception, one which goes unstated but which keeps all the stereotypes thriving:

The idea that salespeople aren't qualified to do anything other than sell.

Ouch. Hurts, doesn't it? But that's the fuel that keeps the fire burning. We're viewed as having no particular specialty. We didn't have to study law or medicine to do what we're doing. Nor did we have to develop an artistic talent.

And the talent we do have, as this book displays, has so many diverse components to it that it's generally hard to understand. But know this: It is indeed a talent. It calls upon one's intellect, intuition, psychological acuity, communication skills, inner fortitude, interpersonal sensitivity, and much, much more.

So go a little easier on us, will ya? We're usually harmless. And a few of us are even really nice people!

How "WE" Envision "YOU"

This isn't complicated: We Love You!

We're grand humanists, salespeople are. We love all of humanity without judgment or hesitation, hence our will to engage with them in the vast flow of commerce that unites us all.

Okay, fine, I'm trying too hard to tip the balance and make you guys feel guilty. The truth is, we do love you guys. And we have your best interests at heart. Screwing people over doesn't make people – even *salespeople* – feel good at all, unless they're cold-hearted sociopaths.

That said, I'll go ahead and admit it:

We do have an opinion or two about the average customer. Generally speaking, salespeople like to joke about how the customer uses their power to their advantage. For example, we might be cold-calling a new prospect, only to find ourselves berated, shrunken down, and humiliated by the voice on the other end.

Then, for the sake of piecing together what remains of our dignity, we'll go ahead and joke that the voice on the phone probably belonged to some pimple-faced nerdy guy who's so short he has to jump off the ground to throw away trash in the trash can.

So sue us, all right?! As I've been trying to make clear: We're only human.

And although we love you, we make fun of you at times.

How "WE" Envision "US"

Oh, this is an easy one.

We salespeople tend to think of ourselves in grounded, sober, highly realistic and self-critical terms. Accordingly, we look at ourselves as handsome, beautiful, brilliant, morally perfect, and extremely popular!

In our own minds, each of us not only thinks we are the greatest salesperson in the world, but also the greatest PERSON in the world – period. We pat ourselves on the back for giving part of our incomes to charity...regardless of whether or not we do. We regard ourselves with pride for our glowing resumes...ignoring the five-year gaps and slightly "adjusted" GPAs.

We are, in essence, the height of perfection, God's gift to humanity, and the most awesome force yet discovered in the entire known universe.

Now please sign the purchase and sales agreement.

The Five Most Common Types Of Salespeople

Whenever you're out there in the world of commerce, playing your dutiful role as a consumer, you're bound to bump into a salesperson. Maybe you're out buying shoes, or a car, or a new TV – or maybe you're buying something more service-oriented, like an ad campaign from a digital media agency. Whatever it is, somewhere along the way, some salesperson will be pushing the limits. That salesperson may be on the other end of the phone, or standing right in front of you, or hiding behind layers of emails and computerized message forms, but rest assured that he or she is there somewhere, eager to play a part in your buying experience.

After a massive amount of intensive research, I have discovered the <u>Five Most Common Types of Salespeople</u> that exist across every imaginable sales scenario. Fortunately for me, there weren't a million Most Common Types, as I really wasn't up for writing an endless book.

As it turns out, despite the vast differences among all products, the similarities among the people selling them are rather striking. In fact, I'm willing to bet some cash that you're about to "bump into" somebody you already know in the pages that follow.

So let's go meet some salespeople...

THE SLICK SALESPERSON

Now, I don't know about you, but when I hear the word "slick," I instantly think negative thoughts. Slick, to me, sounds like it's all about polish, all about surface, with no real depth or nuance underneath.

CHEAP CAR
4
SALE!!
$15,000
OR
LESS
All Cars have engine trouble.
No refunds.

However, when I give the matter more thought, I realize that being "slick" has its positive aspects, too. Slick doesn't need to be oily; it can also be smooth. Slick doesn't need to make us think of snakes; it can also make us think of a well-cleaned car.

A famous individual who epitomizes slickness is Bill Clinton. After all, they nicknamed him "Slick Willy." And love him or hate him, we have to acknowledge that Bill Clinton is one of the most popular men in American culture. Even those who think he's full of crap often can't help but admire the skill and confidence with which he slings his crap.

That's the thing about slickness: Although it may repel us on some level, it also has a way of drawing us into its comforting orbit. When the movie "Wall Street" came out in the 80s, everybody knew Gordon Gekko, played by Michael Douglas, was the bad guy – how could we miss THAT, given the sharp way he spoke and his *slicked-back* hair? And yet, rather than dismiss Gordon Gekko, stock traders and other businesspeople turned him into a hero.

This isn't my way of validating cheaters and liars; it's just my way of saying that the slick salesperson has his or her (but historically his) charms and positive attributes.

WHAT THE SLICK SALESPERSON LOOKS LIKE

The slick salesperson probably spends more time attending to his or her appearance than any other kind of salesperson. After all, the slick salesperson is a creature of surfaces: If the watch and rings and hair aren't all SCREAMING with an unmistakable shine, then there's no reason to even attempt being slick.

The shoes are shining, as well. The clothes have been ironed far more frequently than anybody else's in the office. Even the items not worn by the slick salesperson – such as his or her briefcase or cell phone – give off such a strong shine they could be spotted by planes flying overhead.

If a slick salesperson is in the room, then he or she will be drawing in attention. Sure, there may be some other presentable folks around, but this slick contender will be generating gasps of, "Holy moly – *that's some slick piece of work!*"

WHAT IT'S LIKE TO TALK TO A SLICK SALESPERSON

The slick salesperson gets inside your head. The process is so smooth that you may find yourself feeling hypnotized. Let's suppose our slick salesperson is a he. He'll grab your shoulder and look you in the eyes. He'll say to you (with mint in his breath), "I'm so sorry to hear about XYZ..."

"XYZ" might have been a flat tire you dealt with in the morning, or perhaps the untimely passing of your child's hamster, but whatever it is, you will have the slick salesman's sympathy. He may even start to get tears in his eyes, which he'll wipe away with a five-hundred-dollar Versace silk handkerchief.

"I bet you'd like to see our selection," he'll say as though he's a mind-reader.

"Sure," you'll reply.

"That's good," he'll say, not letting go of your shoulder, "because I have a couple of things that I think you'll really appreciate..."

Then he'll lead you around the shop, and you'll never lose track of the guy on account of his wonderful cologne, which envelops you like a cloud. He'll make clean jokes that aren't really funny but that make you laugh on account of his unreal charm. He'll never stutter, and he'll never break eye contact.

By the time you're through with him (or he's through with you), you won't know whether to hug him or punch him.

SLICK SALESPEOPLE can often be found selling Cars, Shoes, and Home Improvement Items (i.e., new windows or carpets).

THE LOUD SALESPERSON

This one speaks for itself, and believe me, SPEAKS is the operative word...

You can hear this guy or gal from all the way across the office. Whereas slickness tends to gravitate toward men, loudness is not known to favor either gender. And the only thing louder than a loud salesperson's voice is his or her LAUGH, which is so overwhelming that it's known to make others contemplate dialing 911.

But there's truly nothing to be alarmed about. The loud salesperson just enjoys cracking jokes, usually ones which bring blushes to the faces of choir girls. In general, the loud salesperson tends to be a "Type A" personality, which is a polite and technical way of saying that if there's air in the room, then they need it all to themselves. It's a common misconception that all salespeople have Type A personalities, but this couldn't be farther from the truth; we're as diverse as any other pool of people. In fact, it's probably the loud salespeople – with their talent for drawing in attention – that created this popular myth.

WHAT THE LOUD SALESPERSON LOOKS LIKE

Does it really matter? Hasn't the part of the brain that uses your eyes shut down by now, being too busy managing the ears?

All kidding aside, these gals and guys don't care what they look like. In fact, they may go around looking all frazzled and haphazard as a stylistic choice: To them, a bit of chaos in one's physical presentation provides the appealing impression of seeming down-to-Earth. Accordingly, with the loud salesperson, you can expect hair that's overdue for a cut, missing buttons, hanging threads, and colors that could stand to be quieter themselves. In many cases, they're overweight, the better to take up more space in any given room. And if they don't smell like alcohol in the office, then stick around for Happy Hour at the neighborhood bar, because chances are they'll be laying it on *real* thick.

WHAT IT'S LIKE TO TALK TO A LOUD SALESPERSON

You: "I'm here to buy some soap..."

Loud Salesperson: "Too Late! We Used It All Up! HAHAHAHAHA!"

You: (fake laugh)

LS: "Just Kidding! Come Here!" (almost wrestles you into a headlock) "We Got Plenty Of Soap! What's It For? Your Private Parts?! HAHAHAHAHA!"

And it kind of goes on that way until everyone collapses from exhaustion.

LOUD SALESPEOPLE can be found selling ANYTHING, including things that human beings never buy!

THE SENSITIVE SALESPERSON

The sensitive salesperson tends to show up in situations where the salesperson-customer encounter requires time and space to unfold. In other words, you're not going to find a sensitive salesperson standing behind a retail counter or doing telemarketing. No, the sensitive salesperson's more likely to be the one selling you your home, your furniture, or your home electronics. They show up in car dealerships, as well.

Places where you won't just show up and then leave.

Places where you need at least an hour or so.

For these venues allow the sensitive salesperson to start opening up about their personal problems. You see, they're not sensitive about YOUR needs; they're sensitive about THEIR needs.

But from the way they talk, you might miss the distinction.

Emotions are their stock in trade. They'll text you photos of their kids...sitting in a dentist chair. The words at the bottom will read: "This procedure cost me a fortune!"

They'll bring you to tears talking about how their

family just lost everything in a recent hurricane, even though the *truth* is they have a 12th cousin who lost a newspaper in the storm.

They'll create an atmosphere not unlike the one in a psychologist's office, where it seems appropriate to share confessions...despite the fact that the salesperson's the only one doing the confessing.

WHAT THE SENSITIVE SALESPERSON LOOKS LIKE

Much like serial killers, these salespeople tend to look just like everybody else.

WHAT IT'S LIKE TO TALK TO A SENSITIVE SALESPERSON

Sensitive Salesperson: "You'll really like this unit...it's...um...excuse me." (wiping tear away)

You: "What is it?"

SS: "I...just...no, it's nothing." (clearing throat) "Sorry. I was just...up all night."

You: "Oh..."

SS: "Yeah, my youngest...she has this...esophagus problem. It's not really serious. Nothing surgery can't handle."

You: "Oh my goodness!"

SS: "No, stop! Don't worry about it! We do so much praying that I'm sure we'll make our bills this month..."

SENSITIVE SALESPEOPLE can be found selling Real Estate, Home Electronics, Furniture, Cars, and Clothing.

THE LAZY SALESPERSON

Hey look, if we were all competent, the world would be a very boring place.

Some salespeople are just lazy. I know it's hard to believe, given the fact that selling calls for assertiveness, energy, and focus. But a lot of salespeople aren't driven by any internal fire; in fact, they may use the fact that salespeople are supposed to be independent as a way to hide out: Since they alone are the ones in charge of getting results, they feel a certain twisted freedom...

A freedom to sit around and do *absolutely nothing*.

When the lazy salesperson is supposed to go door-to-door, he or she ends up asleep in the car. When the lazy salesperson is supposed to sell cell phones, he or she doesn't know how to work them – and definitely hasn't bothered to charge them for the presentation.

More often than not, the lazy salesperson is advanced in age – what others in the industry might call a "dinosaur." They feel they've paid their dues, and all the hard work now falls upon the younger team members.

Unfortunately for them, in the world of selling, unless you're a manager, you have to keep on doing one thing: SELLING!

WHAT THE LAZY SALESPERSON LOOKS LIKE

Generally, the lazy salesperson is disheveled. For the men, this means unshaven. For the women, this means devoid of make-up. In either case, the hair's not combed, the shoes aren't tied, the car doors can't open without garbage spilling out, and the shirts have so many stains on them they look polka-dotted.

And even though it may not have rained in a month, the lazy salesperson will find some way to step in a puddle.

WHAT IT'S LIKE TO TALK TO A LAZY SALESPERSON

Let's say you're the young newbie and the lazy salesperson's your co-worker:

Lazy Salesperson: "Could you call this lead for me? It's a good one."

You: "Sure, we'll split the commission, right?"

LS: (astonished) "What do you mean? It's my lead."

You: "Yeah, but you're asking me to call."

LS: "I've made enough of these calls to last me a lifetime."

You: "Then maybe you should retire!"

LS: (thoughtful) "Good idea." (pause) "Could you call a retirement home for me?"

LAZY SALESPEOPLE sell Ad Space for Newspapers and The Yellow Pages, Cellular Phones, Car Rentals, and <u>Anything</u> Non-Commissioned.

THE "A" PLAYER

This is the cream of the crop. Every pyramid has its peak, and in the sales world, that peak exists in the form of the "A" Player.

Call them "top dogs" or "Alpha dogs." Call them "the top of the food chain." These are the ones most qualified to get the job *and* the ones most qualified to keep it and get promoted. They are proactive, intuitive, great listeners, sharp dressers, models of attractiveness, superb networkers, and lacerating wits. They are the life of the party, and have a story to match each and every occasion. Generally, the others in the office will either have crushes on them or envy them.

Yet in either case, everyone will be happy to be their friend.

WHAT THE "A" PLAYER LOOKS LIKE

Put it this way:

Let's suppose God personally furnished a vat of flawless DNA, then blessed it a trillion times over and

poured it into a mold so it would take on human form.

That's the "A" Player.

They're not only in the sales world. They're your prom queens and kings, your movie stars, your Barbie and Ken dolls. They exist on the border between reality and fantasy. It's not unusual to think one is 40 years old, only to later find out they're actually 70.

WHAT IT'S LIKE TO TALK TO AN "A" PLAYER

You: "Oh man! That was a really good story!"

"A" Player: "Right? And it's true. Every word of it."

You: "Oh, I believe you. So inspiring."

AP: "I appreciate that. Anyway, here's your invoice..."

You: (smiling) "Invoice? For what?"

AP: (big smile) "The transaction we just completed."

You: (pause)

AP: "Oh, I see – you didn't notice! You were so absorbed in my story that you didn't realize it! Congratulations, my friend! You've purchased a luxury jet."

"A" PLAYERS can be found selling Luxury Vehicles, Software, Suits and other High-End Clothing, and Advertising in Upscale Publications.

PART II:
GETTING TO KNOW THE
SALESPERSON

"I've failed over and over and over again in my life, and that is why I succeed"

~ Michael Jordan

☕ *Ernie P.*
Salesman
Flea Market Goods
36 years in sales

Ernie P. operates off the beaten track. Under the radar. Away from the grid. Out where the buses don't run.

Okay – maybe I've gone a little too far.

The point is, Ernie works in flea market sales. His business model is pretty simple: Every other week, slaps an ad in the local newspaper. The ad reads something along the lines of, "I will come over to your house and cart away your unneeded goods for FREE!"

Like clockwork, he always gets a couple of phone calls. Then he goes over there with his pick-up truck and takes away whatever he can. Usually it's a good score, complete with clothes, appliances, toys, books, movies, and albums. Sometimes he doesn't make out so well – like the time when he showed up and the person wanted him to knock down and drive away their fence! (He ended up doing it since he's such a nice guy. He had to pull up to a nearby forest and toss the fence piece into the woods, which was probably a felony of some kind.)

Once Ernie's stock is nice and full – and he's sorted out all the stuff that people wouldn't buy if their lives depended on it – he gets ready for his TWO-DAY workweek. Sure, he put some hours into hauling away the goods, but the real work is all day Saturday and Sunday, at Ernie's local flea market.

He's there from the crack of dawn to the bust of dust, selling whatever he can for cash. Generally, he ends up with a few hundred bucks in his hands, and it's all cash, so maybe the I.R.S. doesn't have to find out about all of it? Who knows!

Anyway, his overhead is like something out of a dream: Thirty-five bucks for the ad, another fifty for gas, and a total of TEN for the flea market tables. He's only out a hundred bucks or so before he can start making a profit. Sure, it's old school, low-tech, down and dirty, and half-illegal, but Ernie's been sustaining this way for decades now. He's the salt of the Earth, this guy. He's arguably among the last of the true, pure salespeople – the ones who are out there hustling without a corporate logo on the wall behind their heads (heck, if Ernie ever had a logo, he'd have to tape it to the side of his truck!).

Now, to be clear: I'm not advocating tax trickery or operating without a retail license (which you can bet Ernie's never even heard of), but I am saying that resourcefulness is an incredible trait for the hardcore salesperson. At base, salespeople are survivors, and in order to survive in this world, you have to cultivate the ability to make it with very little. Cavemen rubbed together two sticks of wood to make fire.

Ernie P. throws an ad in the paper, keeps his truck from breaking down, and has a business that just keeps sustaining.

TAKEAWAY:

Be resourceful! If you have the will to sell, then believe me, the product and the forum aren't too far from your grasp.

CLOSING STRATEGY:

If people bought it before, then they'll buy it again – even if it's used and bruised the second time around. It's all in how it's presented.

☕ *Mildred F.*
Sales
Funeral Caskets
14 years in sales

I have to be honest here:

I had a very hard time understanding what Mildred F. was saying.

I mean, it's not that she was inarticulate or anything. Quite the contrary, the woman was a champion when it came to her vocabulary and pronunciation. But I do have to say that she was talking very quietly. For real – I was sitting there across from her desk, leaning in, going, "Excuse me? Come again? Can you repeat that, please?"

Later on, when I reviewed our discussion on my digital voice recorder, I was able to hear more or less everything...by cranking the volume up real high!

The thing is, Mildred F. works in a funeral home. You have to work very quietly there. I'm not exactly sure why; it's not like the corpses are going to be woken up! But I suppose that in the midst of such emotional seriousness, there's a natural need to maintain a courteous volume.

"Why were you drawn to this business?" I asked her.

"Somebody has to do it," she whispered, staring a hole through me with cold, dark eyes.

"Okay, fine," I said. "But why YOU? I mean, couldn't you have sold wedding cakes? Or nylon curtains?"

"I've always felt this field has more meaning," Mildred said extremely quietly, to the point where I had to lean in halfway across her desk.

And to be honest, I respect her points. Somebody does have to handle funerals. It's not a fun business, but it's a human one. There's no getting around it. And it was hard not to admire Mildred for exposing herself to a level of emotion that's usually only encountered by doctors, emergency workers, and psychologists.

The funeral business is a lot like any other business, with the key distinction being that death makes for gloomy work. But to speak to Mildred F., it's just like anything else. You get used to it. You learn how to address the clients with compassion. You anticipate their questions – like any quality salesperson – and offer them the package most suited for their needs. Since Mildred's business is regulated, she's required to present the pricing options and services in a very specific manner, all while maintaining airtight composure, class, and respectability.

Which is all well and good – but you know me. I still wanted to hear some scandalous stories.

"Any wild tales?" I asked her. "Any days when something crazy happened?"

"Well..." Mildred whispered, showing me something rare for her: a smile. "There was that one time when we buried a man who was a twin. We didn't know his twin brother would show up at the funeral. So when the twin brother walked in..."

Mildred had to stop herself, because she bent over, howling with laughter.

"One of our staff members screamed and ran away! She thought the twin brother was the corpse, walking around!"

Mildred laughed so hard that she started crying. I have to admit, I laughed a lot myself. Come to think of it, I think both of us were still laughing when we said goodbye.

Jeez, I hope Mildred didn't get fired for being too loud!

TAKEAWAY:
Sales work isn't always light or low stakes. Oftentimes the things we sell are of the utmost importance to people's lives.

CLOSING STRATEGY:
Be sensitive to clients who are going through a lot. The more vulnerable they are, the more ethical, courteous, and confidence-inspiring the salesperson has to be.

☕ *Becky P.*
Stripper
Lap Dances
Four months in sales

Let's get something out of the way right off the bat:

Becky is probably not this woman's real name. Heck, who knows if ANY of the names in this section are real?! Anyway, I bring this up because in Becky's profession, it's not wise to use your real name...

For customers have a way of getting attached to strippers-- ahem! I mean "exotic dancers."

Now, it's tempting to say that Becky sells her body...or at least the sight of it. One could also say she sells dancing, which is the key skill she needed to get her job. However, when you get right down to it, Becky distinguishes herself from the others in these pages by selling something less concrete – something that's a part of many, many kinds of sales.

She sells dreams.

In that sense, what she's carting is no different from what Disney's selling, with the obvious difference being that what she sells is for adults only. That said, her job is to expand people's dream lives. She's selling a side of reality that many people feel is off limits or difficult for them.

Where Becky works, however, the fantasy is attainable, as long as you have the cash and keep your politeness about you ('cause bouncers work there, too).

In terms of nuts-and-bolts selling, Becky's most tangible service is a lap dance. To sell a lap dance requires her to actually approach the customers and offer her services. Now, this can make for some tricky navigating, as some of these customers are highly inept and filled with fear. So Becky's job in those cases becomes to act normal even when she can tell the prospect is quaking in his boots.

Meanwhile, in Becky's line of work, getting rejected for a lap dance can generate awkwardness on the client's part, as they think they're hurting the dancer's feelings.

"Like I care!" Becky says. "I'm just in this to make a living. If they don't want a dance, it's not my problem. It's not like I can't go to the next guy and have him pay."

Only don't tell that to the actual customers. Half of them are entertaining fantasies of a deep, long-term relationship.

Again, the product is a fantasy. To dent the fantasy in any way is to risk spoiling the transaction.

Any funny stories from Becky?

"Too many to mention," she says to me. Then, after thinking about it for a moment, she remembers a guy who actually wanted to marry her!

The "courtship" unfolded somewhat gradually, before accelerating into insanity. First, he gave her massive tips. Then he gave her little gift certificates to clothing stores. Next came the expensive jewelry. And then finally one night he got on his knee – right there in the lap dance booth – with a little box holding a ring.

She wanted to snatch it up from that box, but she knew doing so would open up a world of trouble. So she just laughed and told the guy he was hilarious.

He wasn't laughing, however. In fact, he went home crying.

And (fortunately for Becky) he never came back again.

TAKEAWAY:
Fantasies are a crucial aspect of so much of what's available in commerce. Sometimes the physical thing you're selling (i.e., dancing) isn't as important as the mental one (i.e., a dream).

CLOSING STRATEGY:
When selling a fantasy, give as much as you can to keep the illusion intact. But when the client tries to mix fantasy with reality, set boundaries and keep your distance.

☕ *Biff Hannegan*
Specialist
Hunting Supplies
9 years in sales

When I tried explaining to Biff that I intended to keep all the profiled salespeople's names anonymous, I swear he almost reached for a rifle.

"Why?" he screamed. "I'm Biff Hannegan! Not Biff H.! Am I not supposed to be proud of my name?!"

Biff then went on to point out that the use of his full name might help him sell more hunting supplies. Hey, anything's possible – and you won't catch me trying to stop an honest sale.

Biff got into moving hunting supplies late in his teen years, when most of his friends were either going off to college or entering the military. His family didn't have the money for college, his grades weren't good enough for a scholarship, and his sight wasn't quite good enough for him to pass the military's physical exam. That last item was a heartbreaker for Biff, as he would have been a fourth-generation American military serviceman. However, not one to get beaten down by life, he embraced what he felt was the next best thing:

Selling guns.

Whoops! Did I say that? No, no, no. There are plenty of other supplies at Biff's store. Canteens, hunting jackets, bird whistles, little tents, water coolers...and...um...

Guns! Lots and lots of guns.

I'm no psychologist, but I'd go as far as to say that the guns were the main item in Biff's shop. This wasn't only as far as he was concerned, but as far as the customers were concerned as well. Everybody who walked in there only wanted to look at, examine, and talk about the guns.

"Are these guys all hunters?" I asked him.

Shrugging, he said, "Some. Some are just interested in self-defense. Or target shooting."

I was almost afraid to ask him for a funny story, as I got the sneaking suspicion that he'd tell me about somebody blowing their own foot off. However, when that part of the conversation rolled around, Biff said to me, "It was hilarious. I'll never forget it. A guy came in here to go moose hunting. So I showed him some of my more high-powered pieces, but all the fella wanted...was a bow and arrow."

Cracking up with laughter, Biff Hannegan said, "Can you imagine? Hunting down a moose with a bow and arrow?! You can't even see the thing EXPLODE if you go that way!"

I tried to laugh a little, too, but by then I had one eye on the door.

TAKEAWAY:
The Second Amendment is alive and well!

CLOSING STRATEGY:
When you're selling guns, I don't think you need one.

Seems that product moves like hot cakes. But if you want some amateur advice, here you go: Make sure the inventory isn't loaded!

☕ *Angie K.*
Saleswoman
Outbound Telemarketer
3 years in sales

Angie K. was reluctant to get into telemarketing because she didn't want to be (her words) "one of those annoying people who bother people during dinner."

However, once she started working the phones (an emergency move that came about when she lost her waitressing gig), she realized that it wasn't so bad. Very few people were particularly mean; if they didn't want to hear what she was saying, they just hung up the phone. No big deal. It was part of the game. And besides, she always had umpteenth more numbers on her list to call.

What Angie learned very fast in telemarketing was the beauty of a certain principle called the Law of Averages. This law is known to all who work in sales. The basic principle is: The more prospects you approach, the more likely you are to convert some into clients.

In fact, the Law of Averages dictates that you can't hit zero if you work enough prospects.

Now, naturally, some people just aren't cut out to sell, and might not finesse their voice, pitch, and professionalism to a point where they can convert. In addition, although the Law of Averages is a very real thing, some products/salespeople can stir up different conversion rates from others.

In Angie's case, the product is phone, cable, and Internet services. Since her leads are "warm" – meaning she calls the numbers of people who've already expressed some interest in her company's services in the past – she can generally expect to sell between three and five new service packages a day. With the commissions she earns, she makes a decent living, but it's not all as easy as it sounds.

Sometimes natural cold streaks emerge, and two weeks will drag by with spotty sales. Other times, she ends up working such a high call volume that her vocal cords get strained, and she finds herself at home nursing hot tea and cough drops. Given the unpredictable nature of the work, she's reluctant to spend money on leisure unless she's got plenty of cash in the bank.

"You never know in this economy," she says. "I'm lucky to have a good gig, but it's definitely a case where I have to show up and perform to keep my income healthy."

Asked if she recalls any instances that were noteworthy, dramatic, or amusing, she shares a story about a sale that was unfolding on a golden level. The prospect was buying everything on the menu. Every add-on, every offer, every detail drew out an enthusiastic, "YES!"

Angie sat there clicking on her keyboard, wondering how in the world the Law of Averages had led her to such an eager, carefree buyer.

Then the next thing she knew, the voice on the

phone changed:

"WHO IS THIS?" the new voice demanded.

When Angie explained who she was, the voice explained to her that she had just spent twenty minutes speaking with her father...who had just that morning been released from a mental health facility.

"He has dementia," the woman explained. "Now please cancel our whole order!"

Naturally, Angie deleted everything, unsure of whether to laugh or cry.

TAKEAWAY:
Money in the bank isn't money in the bank until it's actually money in the bank. So be smart and save, 'cause there are always peaks and valleys.

CLOSING STRATEGY:
The Law of Averages is a reassuring aspect of reality. Knock on enough doors, and some are bound to open. You just need the persistence and bravery to knock, and the right moves once the door is opened.

🦐 *Lee F.*
Agent
Insurance
3 years in sales

When it comes time to close an insurance deal,
Lee F. sweeps in with full preparation. He's not just good
because he's knowledgeable. He's not just good because
he's experienced.

No, he's good because he's a role-player.

Hold on, hold on. This has nothing to do with
video games. Moreover – calm down! – this doesn't
involve freaky bedroom stuff, either.

At least not as far as I know...

Anyway, what I mean by "role-playing" is,
Lee acts out scenarios – typically in partnership with
a fellow salesperson – in which the roles of buyer and
seller are both played out. That way, he gets a chance to
be on both sides of the equation. He puts himself in the
buyer's shoes, gets accustomed to thinking the buyer's
thoughts, and comes up with the natural questions,
concerns, and objections that the buyer would present.

It's a pretty sharp idea, actually.

In some schools of marketing, before a product
is ever developed, it's advisable to draw up a deep and
detailed psychological profile of the ideal customer.
It may sound a little silly at first – creating a fictional
character in the all-business realm of sales – but in fact
it's incredibly practical and useful.

For after all, fiction follows life.

And the "character" whom one comes up with before marketing a product allows one to craft and perfect the product with all of the character's concerns, tastes, preferences, and interests in mind.

Getting back to Lee F. and the value of role-playing: The advantages of putting oneself in the buyer's shoes are limitless. In fact, a lousy salesperson will think of the buyer as naive or dumb, never empathizing with him or her, yet concentrating on making the sale just the same.

But mentally journeying into the buyer's space allows sellers a chance to see the transaction from both sides and accordingly up their game.

However – importantly – there are always situations in which although you might know everything about what the buyer wants and where the buyer's coming from, additional factors to the transaction limit your effectiveness. In Lee's field, insurance, one such factor is his own inability to approve a given client's coverage. He can make the sale, but the ultimate coverage decision is up to another party. During one memorable instance, this became a problem:

"I had a husband and wife that I was putting together a long-term care plan in place for...After two meetings, the paperwork was signed and submitted to underwriting for process. When the case came back to me from underwriting, the wife was approved; however, the husband was not."

Ouch. Uh oh. Suddenly poor Lee found himself at

the center of a family drama...

He goes on: "When I contacted the husband and broke the news to him, he was extremely upset and wanted to cancel his wife's policy, along with a full refund of his money. I calmly asked if I could stop by his office to drop everything off, and he said, 'Yes.'"

Naturally, Lee's no quitter, and his true goal was to save the sale.

Prior to stopping by the client's office, Lee collected himself. This was a tough one, no doubt about it. How do you manage to role-play when you're positive the client himself can't be sold (even though his wife already was)?

Lee went in there and did his best. The discussion was far from brief; it went on for quite some time. In the end, Lee had to accept reality:

The husband allowed him to keep the wife as a client!

Hey, sometimes in the sales world, you do meet guys who could sell ice to Eskimos in the wintertime.

TAKEAWAY:
Though you can know your clientele like the back of your hand, you can't always control every situation. So when the going gets tough, the tough get creative.

CLOSING STRATEGY:
Role-play, role-play, role-play. If you can't see the world through your clients' eyes, you'll only manage to exist in one half of the transaction. Masterful sales people

expand their perception.

🝮 *Teddy F.*
Product Specialist
Cars
20 years in sales

Teddy F. was working in the landscaping business. One day, while he was hosing down some bushes, a buddy of his walked by wearing a six-hundred-dollar suit. Teddy had to control himself from spraying water all over the place.

"Whoa!" he said to his pal. "What have YOU been up to?"

"Selling cars," the guy said in an intense, raspy voice.

A chill flew up Teddy's spine. He dropped the hose on the ground and told his boss he was quitting. No more landscaping for him; the car business seemed to be where it was at.

Twenty years later, that continues to remain the case.

Teddy's career high point came when he harnessed his sales skills toward the cause of selling cars to an entire family: mother, father, three daughters, and a son.

They all walked onto the lot together. The salespeople started trading glances, wondering who these folks were. After all, they looked kind of disheveled, and there were so many of them that it was kind of hard to know where to begin.

Seeing that none of his coworkers were willing to take the bait, Teddy straightened his tie and walked on over. "Can I help you?" he asked.

Nodding, one of them said, "Today is your lucky day..."

Teddy had no way of knowing how true those words would prove to be. They wanted SIX cars! Not only that, but they're loyal clients, so they continue to rotate back to him for new cars every year or so.

Teddy attributes his ability to close to his honesty and his ability to build real trust. In that remarkable situation, even though the family walked in willing to buy, they might have been turned off had no one given them the time of day. Teddy's awareness of his own ability to treat them well and present them with a truthful package allowed him to step in and investigate.

And the result no doubt belongs in a record book somewhere.

TAKEAWAY:
Don't judge a book by its cover. Don't keep your distance just because your coworkers think it's fashionable to do so. Know that the higher your ethics are, the more you will stand out.

CLOSING STRATEGY:
Be a good person, be yourself, and treat people how you would want to be treated.

🏆 Naima C.
Sales Coordinator
Enterprise Software
1 year in sales

After stating that she fell into sales "by accident," Naima goes on to describe the sales realm as "so so" and say she wouldn't recommend the field to friends and family members. Then, in a staggering reversal, she labels herself as successful and cites (if I understood her correctly!) a 100% closing rate!

Sometimes nonchalance equals power, I suppose.

To hear Naima describe it, all she has to do is lay out the ROI to be gained from her product, and a healthy close is well within reach. If her clients are happy, then she's happy...and she goes home and sleeps like a baby.

There's a strong lesson here: The successful salesperson doesn't have to be go-go-go. On the contrary, he or she can function at an optimum level by simply remaining chill.

In fact, Naima didn't even bat an eyelash when describing her largest success:

"I closed the largest deal in company history which is over eight figures. I'm proud because it was a HUGE commission check and it gave me a lot of visibility with my company and may fast track me to the next level."

It took me a few moments to recover from

that piece of information. To be honest, I was kind of angling for a way to get some of that commission money for myself. But then I pulled myself together and remembered there was a book to be written.

Hoping for a little reprieve from all this talk about shattered records and swimming pools full of cash, I asked her if she had a funny, dramatic, or otherwise memorable tale to share from her career. Here's what she hit me with in return:

She had an initial meeting set up with a prospect – a fellow female. The two of them went out for dinner in the evening. On the way back to Naima's car, they sensed the presence of an outsider...paying attention to them...

The next thing Naima knew, she saw a gun.

"We were robbed at gunpoint for our purses, and they took the car to boot."

What a nightmare! Not only was it terribly scary, but it surely killed the deal, right?

Wrong!

Naima didn't even have to sell this lady anymore. As of that horrifying incident, they had a natural bond, and the customer felt a reflexive inclination to do business with her. Naima even kind of suspected that the lady felt bad because it was Naima's car that got stolen, but whatever her core motives were, the business relationship remained strong and steady.

After all, she closes at A HUNDRED PERCENT!

TAKEAWAY:

It's the quiet ones you have to watch. Sometimes the slick loudmouth ain't got nothing on the casual operator.

CLOSING STRATEGY:

What strategy?! Did you hear what I said?! A HUNDRED PERCENT! As long as she's breathing, she's selling. (Nah, it's essentially all about the bond or commonalities you share with your prospect or client.)

☕ Carmen V.
Account Director
Advertising
5 years in sales

Prior to going into sales, Carmen did a little research. She learned something that often comes up in discussions of the sales profession – namely that it's an arena where you have the ability to make unlimited amounts of money.

Talk about a glass-half-full mentality!

The person who couldn't ever tolerate sales would see the lack of a predictable salary as a giant red flag. It takes a true natural – a true native to the sales realm – to see potential where others might see instability.

So Carmen exited the accounting world, whereupon she sold make-up for a living. Nowadays, she sells advertising. Since she has a passion for the product, she describes the closing process as an "infectious" one, whereby the buyer can't help but be ignited by what she's presenting. It's a matter of articulating the ROI within the context of the buyer's budget, and the rest tends to flow like water from a fountain.

Interestingly, when asked to cite a high point of career pride, Carmen says, "The time that I sold the smallest deal of my career."

I had to take a moment to wrap my head around that one. I mean, did the customer end up marrying her

91

or something...?

As it turned out, even though the sale itself was small, the company that made the buy was a brand new purchaser. For Carmen, that meant providing a great deal of education and schmoozing: She had to really reach inside for as much knowledge, helpfulness, and personability as she could muster. Since she's not a fan of the whole stereotype about salespeople talking nonstop, this wasn't necessarily her standard closing strategy.

Regardless, it worked out in the end, and Carmen got something that is oftentimes sweeter than money: A sense of fulfillment.

Armed with this capacity to convert brand new business, Carmen found herself on the receiving end of an invitation from another prospect. He wanted to take her out for drinks, for the expressed purpose of getting to know her and her firm.

She accepted the invitation, and as the night went on, Carmen found herself in an open mic comedy club. She did a double-take when she saw the prospect climb up on stage and get behind the microphone.

For a moment, she couldn't help but wonder if she was on a hidden-camera reality show.

Then, for 15 minutes (which felt like 15 hours), the prospect proceeded to "clown on" Carmen – making her the target of his comedic onslaught. The entire audience was in stitches, and although Carmen was more surprised than amused, she at least kept a smile on her face.

Which was good, because the whole shtick, while not a reality show, was a preplanned test.

As it turned out, this prospect always did this kind of stuff. His rule of thumb: If you don't laugh, he doesn't buy.

Fortunately, Carmen managed to laugh...even though she'd find the whole thing funnier in hindsight.

TAKEAWAY:
In the world of sales, the money is infinite...and so are the surprises!

CLOSING STRATEGY:
Shut up and listen to your prospect/client, 'cause you'll learn a lot. And also: Laugh your way to the bank (without losing yourself or your integrity).

🍵 *Omar C.*
Mobile Phone Specialist
Electronics/Cell Phones
12 years in sales

Omar started his career in sales in the same place that most of us do:

By working as a barber.

Okay, you got me. Never mind. Most salespeople don't start off as barbers – obviously. However, one day Omar was trimming a customer's hair, when one of his fellow barbers walked over and cried, "Omar! What are you and I doing here?! The world of sales awaits us like a seductive mistress in the cool purple of the night!"

How could Omar resist such a pitch?

The next thing he knew, he was pushing electronic items and cell phones. His closing strategy is as simple and direct as his decision to become a salesman in the first place:

"Look them in the eyes and ask for the business."

Wait a second – THAT'S IT? What if they say no?!

"Ask why."

I assume you're not supposed to break eye contact when asking why.

If all of this sounds menacing, we can all go ahead and just relax. Omar's a perfectly nice and civil fellow – so nice that he actually had the patience and compassion to walk a woman in her 80s through the use of her very first cell phone.

The customer had no clue how the phone worked, and even asked Omar how it connected to the wall. Patiently (and with full, unblinking eye contact), Omar showed her the owner's manual. Over the course of two hours, he walked her through every detail of how to use the phone. By the time they were done, she could have BUILT her own phone, let alone used one.

So enormous was the customer's gratitude that she wrote a kind letter to Omar's boss, as well as his boss's boss (as for his boss's boss's boss, we can't be sure, because that becomes a spiritual matter involving God). In addition, the customer came back in to Omar's place of work to give him a fresh homemade batch of cookies.

A very nice gesture, and it at least proved that she knows how to use an oven.

This is not to say that every deal in the cell phone sphere ends with heartwarming letters, homemade cookies, and a spot in the customer's will. Quite the contrary, Omar has encountered his share of shady characters, as well.

"When I first started selling cell phones, the industry was a little relaxed, and a person really didn't have to provide much information to get service."

(Speaking of which: Who WAS That Old Lady?!)

"So there was a high-profile group of organized crime members that would come to me with their aunt's ID, grandmother's ID, sisters, et cetera, so that the phones were not in their names..."

Omar sold to these fellas for three months. Then

one day he was watching the news, and saw they all got busted by way of wiretaps on their phones.

And the worst part is, Omar didn't even get any cookies.

TAKEAWAY:
Put down the barber's sheers, read the old lady the whole phone manual, and sell phones to gangsters. Duh!
CLOSING STRATEGY:
Look. Them. In. The. Eye. They don't like it? Whatever. Keep...looking...and ask for their business.

Norm L.
Chief Sales Officer
Medical Devices (X-ray & CAT scan machines)
24 years in sales

Formerly a components salesman – and a bartender before that – Norm makes the case that persistence (in addition to the ever valuable trait of proving ROI) is what keeps the salesperson afloat. He presumes that some people look at those in the sales world and see a bunch of actors pretending to care, but he doesn't let this perception get to him, for he knows what's true at the end of the day. Better to keep your head down and press forward rather than allow yourself to get eaten up by naysayers.

It was this very sense of perseverance that allowed Norm to step into a high-pressured presentation before the board of directors of a hospital group containing seven hospitals. His job? To not only lay out the ROI, but to present a detailed, well-reasoned case as to why they should hire his company and not the competition.

The grilling went on for two long hours.

And as prepared as he was, Norm simply did not have all the answers they were after. In the end, they had to break the bad news to him: They weren't going to go with his company.

Norm's shoulders slumped. Win some, lose some, he supposed. Not one to let defeat dampen his spirit, he did the professional thing and sent a follow-up email to each of the 12 board members, thanking them for the opportunity to give his presentation.

Ninety days slipped by, and Norm forgot about the whole thing.

Then, out of the blue, Norm's phone rang. It was an assistant to one of the board members. The board member wanted to meet with Norm. When Norm went in, he learned that the member he was meeting with happened to be the group's treasurer.

The treasurer informed Norm that he had indeed won their business.

The lesson was a clear one: Never give up, never back down, and always remember that the tides have a way of turning.

More inspirational still was a memorable encounter Norm had when selling emergency room equipment. He came upon a burn victim who – despite having burns over 9/10 of his body – was extremely lucid and coherent.

He kept making jokes at Norm's expense, to the point where the hospital staffers were doubled over with laughter. Norm couldn't help but laugh himself, but the question was nagging at him: "HOW is this guy able to stay so witty and together when in so much pain?"

As it turned out, the burn victim was a stand-up comedian.

Persistence is a great thing, indeed.

TAKEAWAY:

Say it with me one more time: Never give up, never back down, and always remember that the tides have a way of turning.

CLOSING STRATEGY:

Present the information while treating all the prospects/ clients the same way, as if they've already bought something from you.

🐝 *Sheila M.*
Sales Specialist
Diamonds/Jewels/High-end Time Pieces
4 years in sales

Sometimes one's sales job has a source close to home: One's family.

One day, you see, Sheila's husband asked her to help out with his business. Her answer was a natural yes, for she can close like nobody's business. Her strategy?

"Mapping back to the reasons why they walked into the store in the first place."

Not a bad idea. The wisdom of that strategy resides in the fact that within every purchase is a motive of some kind. This corresponds with the value of role-playing – and figuring out where the customer's coming from. If you can just tune in to what they're after, you're putting yourself on very secure footing when it comes to helping them grasp it.

Moreover, this principle pertains to clients from all walks of life. On one memorable occasion, Sheila sold a set of earrings to a very well-known basketball player. Not only did the guy drop a lot of money ("drop" being the operative word, considering how tall he stood above the counter), he also turned into a repeat customer, and told all his buddies/teammates to shop at Sheila's place, as well.

Of course, every high in the sales world can find a low to balance it out – and in Sheila's case, this meant being robbed at gunpoint.

The thieves stole every last jewel in the store, then capped off the crime by tying her up and locking her in the safe. The good news was, they'd triggered the silent alarm during the robbery.

The bad news was, it took six hours for help to arrive and the safe to be unlocked.

TAKEAWAY:
You never know who's walking in the door, and the more luxurious the item, the more it will appeal to the wealthy...and the desperate.

CLOSING STRATEGY:
Know why they walked in there to begin with. Don't lose sight of that factor, as it's clay you can use to mold a successful sale.

🖲 *Richie H.*
Sales Development Specialist
Multi-level Marketing (MLM)
2 years in sales

Dog walking wasn't cutting it for Richie.

Being an office coordinator wasn't cutting it for Richie.

So one day, when a Multi-level Marketing rep presented him with a pitch, he nodded his head and said, "Okay. Let's go."

Richie adheres to the mode of thought that says salespeople are really just educators. As far as he's concerned, he's not in a position to make anyone's decisions for them. He simply presents information which allows them to make their own choices.

Since those choices often are to Richie's benefit, he considers himself to be good at what he does.

Which is not to say it's always been an effortless process. When Richie got started, he was at the mall working on recruiting new candidates. About a hundred people shook their heads and said, "No." Just as Richie was about to pack it in and call it a day, a woman approached him and asked him what he was doing.

It was like a sign from the universe.

Launching back into sales mode, Richie explained the product and how it worked. Within 15 minutes, the lady signed up.

Nowadays, she's the Number 1 producer on

Richie's team.

After Richie got the ball rolling and got situated as a team lead, one of his team members asked him to give a presentation to a group of potential customers/ sellers at the team member's home. It all sounded fine and dandy...except for the fact that the guy lived in a pretty rough part of town.

So when Richie went over there, his nerves were doing a number on him.

In any event, the presentation unfolded as planned. Part of the way through, a knock landed on the door. When someone opened it, four guys in black – all of them wearing ski masks – stormed in, snatched up the owner, and stuffed him into a van that was waiting outside.

Needless to say, everybody went NUTS. Yelling. Screaming. Calling 911.

Then one of the bandits came back in! He wasn't wearing his mask anymore. One of the prospects put up a lethal defense: swiping at the guy over and over with a tennis racket.

The tennis racket assault went on for about three minutes.

Finally, amidst all the commotion, the intruder yelled out that it was all just a joke!

The "kidnapping" had been part of the homeowner's bachelor party.

TAKEAWAY:
Who says Multi-level Marketing isn't a hotbed of

excitement and suspense?!

CLOSING STRATEGY:
Give them the information and let them decide whether or not to become a customer. Or salesman. Or both! Hey, it's MLM! Anything goes!

☕ *Chet W.*
Sales Director
Snake Oil
57 years in sales

My examination of Chet W. was, in a word, frightening.

Chet didn't want to talk about salespeople. Didn't want to discuss his personal history. In fact, I'm not entirely convinced that he was human.

The only quantifiable detail he gave me was that he's been in sales for 57 years, but the problem was he looked no older than 28.

"How do you account for that?" I asked him.

Smiling at me with perfect teeth, he said, "It's the snake oil."

The snake oil was Chet's signature product. He drove around North America with polished cans of it all packed together in the trunk of his car. He claimed rubbing the oil on your skin would reverse your aging process.

"Some of my clients are over 500 years old," he told me.

It was getting late when I spoke to him. We were at a strange roadside diner in the middle of nowhere, and I started to get the feeling that I had crossed into some other dimension.

"You have," Chet told me, reading my mind. "You're in a dimension where all salespeople sell snake oil – and ARE EVIL!"

Then Chet turned into a dragon and flew right toward me.

Fortunately I got out of there before things got ugly.

TAKEAWAY:

There's no such thing as snake oil! What does that even mean? Not all salespeople are evil; in fact, most of us are far from it. So RELAX!

CLOSING STRATEGY:

You do realize that was make believe, don't you? Why would you even want to know the closing strategy, you big silly?!

☕ *Tony J.*
Sr. Account Manager
Electro-Mechanical Passive Components
17 years in sales

Tony J. embodies one of the most common traits of successful salespeople: He's *aggressive.* This doesn't mean he poses a physical threat to anyone (at least not as far as I know), but that he'll do whatever it takes to close a deal.

He got into the sales game when person after person told him he was a natural hustler, so selling might just be his thing. At the time, he was working as a personal trainer, but rather than help his clients to improve their bodies, he spent all day trying to get them to upgrade their membership packages at the gym. It wasn't long before the clients started recommending that new line of work to Tony. Usually they were screaming when they did so.

Before settling on electro-mechanical passive components, Tony sold cars, telephone books, and even staffing. He's developed a real strong nose for "tire kickers," those people who spend their whole lives window shopping, wondering how much that doggie in the window costs. Once he sniffs out the tire kickers, he kicks them to the curb and focuses on the true potential closes.

That's how he maintains a high closing rate, complete with strong commission checks and a solid position at his company.

Tony says salespeople are perceived "as terrible listeners, out for themselves."

Which was a strange thing to say, since I'd only asked him how his day was. Jeez, was the guy even listening to me?

He also says people bear the misconception that salespeople would sell their own children just to score a good close. He made it perfectly clear that he draws the line at his nieces and nephews, and would never sell one of his own offspring.

Tony J.'s proudest moment in sales came when he had a prospect who flat-out told him he'd NEVER buy from him or his company. Not one to give up easily, Tony did some intense research, tied the prospect's specific business strategy back his own company's services, and managed to finally sell the guy. It took six months, but time is irrelevant when you've decided to never give up.

The low point of Tony's sales career came when he was in the staffing industry. One client needed help staffing his liquor promotion company. His requirement? To fill the staff with "stripper-type" women.

So Tony hit the street, going to strip clubs as a recruiter. Naturally, the gig seemed incredibly positive at first, until one club owner spotted Tony trying to steal his staff members. A great big shadow fell over Tony. He looked up and saw a couple of bouncers. He not only got thrown out of the club, but he got banned for life.

If you go in there today, there's even a picture of Tony on the wall. The words "Stripper Thief" are printed under it in golden glitter.

Low points aside, Tony loves the sales profession. In fact, the only thing he thinks is missing from it is an intuitive Customer Relationship Management (CRM) system that helps salespeople identity clients and prospects based on their physical features.

You know, in case the salesperson ever forgets their names.

TAKEAWAY:
Be aggressive and don't give up, even if it means hectoring leads for six months or walking into seedy back-alley strip clubs.

CLOSING STRATEGY:
Hone in on the true prospects and leave the tire kickers out on the curb!

🍵 *Brandon S.*
Consultant
Management Consulting
8 years in sales

"I love money," says Brandon S., declaring himself to be someone who doesn't beat around the bush.

Accordingly, since he loves the dough, Brandon soars when things are high and crashes when things are low. (Sorry about that – Don't mean to rhyme all the time!)

Brandon doesn't have any specific closing strategy that he can nail down, but he's good when it comes to being a member of the client's team. He gets to know them. Becomes a part of their world. Inserts himself into their culture. Sometimes he even shows up at their houses on the weekends and makes them breakfast.

All kidding aside, here's a guy who will do what it takes to close. And the more the client thinks of him as one of their own – as opposed to a distant, separate entity – the more likely they are to trust him and keep the dollars flowing his way.

Which is not to say that cash is Brandon's only motivator. He also says one's performance against one's peers, one's progress within a company, and one's title are good indicators of success.

Then, because he just can't help himself, he mentions MONEY again.

When it comes to how others view salespeople,

two misconceptions jump out at Brandon. The first is that they're slimy, sketchy, and uncaring about the organizations they represent. The second is that they're not hard workers. On the contrary, Brandon says top salespeople are often not only ethical and credible, but are often the first ones to show up at the office when it opens, and the last ones to leave when it closes.

And no, that's not because they're stealing any cash from the safe!

One day, out in the field, Brandon found himself in a predominantly female office. The man whom he was meeting with pulled him aside and informed him of a brewing situation. Turned out he was about to fire another guy, and he was worried the guy would physically explode and create a dangerous scenario.

Brandon, being the only other available male on the scene, was recruited to provide reinforcements.

So not only are salespeople often ethical and hardworking – sometimes they're also superheroes!

Or – okay, fine – that's probably going too far.

They're just *heroes*. We'll leave it at that.

TAKEAWAY:
Ain't no shame in going after the bucks, so long as you don't sell your soul.

CLOSING STRATEGY:
Become one of them. This is particularly easy if you're selling to your own parents.

🖋 *Craig H.*
Sr. Account Executive
Tech Research
15 years in sales

Craig H. got into sales by way of being part of a family business. When asked if he considers himself to be a strong closer, he says, "Yes, I've learned to ask for the business."

For a second there I thought he meant the *family business!*

When it comes to closing, Craig says it's first and foremost about proving that the value of whatever you're offering is greater than the price (always tricky for those fellas who sell ice to Eskimos in the wintertime). In addition, you have to get personal and build a rapport, which helps to build up trust.

He says that salespeople are stereotyped as opportunists and swindlers with an over-aggressive streak. Then he hands me back my wallet, winks at me, and says, "You should be more careful, pal," and claps me really hard on the shoulder.

Nah, Craig's a good guy. He once got a client to sign blind simply because the client believed in HIM. It wasn't even about the product in that case. Which was a relief, since the product was a life-sized poster of Don Knotts.

No stranger to danger on the job, Craig once walked onto a construction site cold at six a.m. And by cold, I meant they weren't expecting him; the weather was actually quite pleasant. He was making his living prospecting construction subcontractors at the time.

But little did he know that the place had just been robbed the night before.

The subcontractors pulled him into a room, shined a hot, bright light into his eyes, and began interrogating him. When he explained to them that their insurance would more than cover their losses (as he'd gladly sell them new supplies well below their anticipated replacement cost), they backed off and became overjoyed.

Moreover – and more important – the guys bought everything Craig was selling.

So what's the moral of the story?

Sometimes you not only sell to a customer in need – you sell to a customer who was Actually Just Robbed of WHAT YOU'RE SELLING.

That's what I call good fortune for everyone involved.

TAKEAWAY:
The good guys often win.

CLOSING STRATEGY:
Convince them it's worth it. Convince them YOU'RE worth it.

☕ Jay W.
Executive Recruiter
Recruiting/Staffing
12 years in sales

At the hospital, when Jay W. was born, his mother and father asked the doctor, "Is it a girl? Is it a boy?"

Shaking his head, the doctor said back, "You've just had a *natural born hustler.*"

Objections bounce off Jay like bullets bounce off Superman. Moreover, he works hard enough during the qualification process to keep any objections to a minimum. When you lay that kind of groundwork, it's less about "selling" somebody than it is about "fulfilling an apparent need."

His closing strategy involves a little trial and error. Like a fisherman, he drops his line in one part of the water, and then slides it over to another part. In the process, he figures out where the bites might come from. By determining the client's absolute limits – what they are absolutely unwilling to buy – he is able to focus in on what's possible, and then turn that possibility into a reality.

How does Jay W. measure success? Simple: When the time he spends on deals goes down, and the income he makes from deals goes up. The epitome of this measuring system came when Jay made almost $30,000 from a company that simply wanted him to verify the qualifications of a job candidate THEY ALREADY KNEW ABOUT!

In other words, they sent Jay the guy's resume and said, "We really like him. Should we hire him?"

Jay sat with the guy for a little while, called back the hiring office, and said, "Yeah, sure. Hire him."

The thirty grand was wired forty seconds later.

TAKEAWAY:

I'm sorry – what were we just talking about? I'm a little distracted by that last story!

CLOSING STRATEGY:

Eliminate the impossible so you can focus on the possible and bag the deal.

🕯 *Joseph T.*
Sales Director
Paper Products
22 years in sales

Joey T. doesn't mess around when it comes to closing. Does he throw stardust in anyone's eyes? No. Does he try to draw anyone's attention away from the product cost? No.

Joey T. just focuses on three...little...letters: R...O...I.

When you buy from him, you can expect returns. If you don't get returns – then don't buy from him again. What does he care? Joey T. ain't out to make life hard for anyone.

His mentality is just as simple when it comes to measuring success. How does he do it? By observing "the size of my commission check."

If it's big, he's a winner. If it's small, he's a loser. *Forget about it!*

He knows there are people out there who says salespeople are dumb and money hungry. He's heard the talk about salespeople not caring, and trying to sell you everything under the sun. But does he let that keep him up at night?

What do you think?! Get outta here with the negativity! *Show some respect to Joey T.!*

Do you know how smart Joey T. is? Well, I'll tell ya. One time he got a family-owned hotel to stop buying products from their own *cousin* and instead buy from him. How'd he pull off such a stunt?

Simple.

He pointed out that the cousin was overcharging them. And he made it clear that his return on investment profile would land them in a whole new league.

The hotel expanded. Business exploded. And now *Joey T.'s* like a cousin to them.

It's not all wine and roses, though. For example, Joey T. will never forget the time when he found himself selling products to a mob-owned restaurant. The boss was staring a hole right through him. For some reason the boss thought Joey T. was a rat from another mob family.

For hours, the boss just sat there, grilling him.

"You sure you don't ever make drops for Jimmy Mashed Potatoes?" he asked.

"No!" Joey screamed. "I never *even heard of* Jimmy Mashed Potatoes!"

Pointing a finger, the boss said, "Oh, you trying to be a tough guy now?"

Joey T. was certain he would die, but maybe the pressure and adrenaline upped his game, for not only did he earn the gangster's trust...

But he actually bagged the deal.

On his way out of that place, guess who walked in? If you said "the FBI," you'd be right! They busted the joint – started arresting people. Joey T. found himself in handcuffs, getting interrogated until roosters began crowing.

When they learned he was clean, they let him go.

'Cause the thing about Joey T. is: He always gets out of jams in one piece. *Forget about it!*

TAKEAWAY:
If there were more Joey T.'s around the neighborhood, everything would get a whole lot better, I'll tell you that much.

CLOSING STRATEGY:
Weren't you even listening, pal? R – O – I. If you can't provide, you'll be denied.

🍵 *Andre S.*
Real Estate Agent
Real Estate
4 years in sales

Do yourself a favor, will ya?

Don't read this section too close to bedtime.

'Cause the story of Andre S. isn't ordinary. Sure, it all seems ordinary on the surface, but lurking not far beneath are some dark memories that would make Stephen King start to shriek in terror.

Andre is a man of decent character and sound philosophy. On the question of how he closes, he cites a need to provide the client with everything they require so a clear purchasing decision can be made.

That all sounds normal enough, doesn't it?

In addition, when I asked Andre how he measures success, he stated with maturity and centeredness, "The number of houses that I sell."

Ah, yes. Very mainstream. Nothing to trouble one's soul.

And then Andre thought it would be a good idea to tell the story of his most unusual sale...

The setting was a giant house, in a sought-after part of town. He was scheduled to show the home to a family. It had been on the market for four months, and was said to be vacant.

Indeed, when they got there, the house *was* vacant. So Andre did his job, guiding the family from room to room and gracing them with an extraordinary amount of useful information.

At which point they decided to take a little stroll... down into the basement...

It seemed like a normal basement at first. Until, that is, the *shrieking* started.

The screams came from a far corner. There, on a bare mattress, was a grown man who was bleeding profusely.

Naturally, the family decided it would be a good idea to run.

As for Andre – for reasons known only to him – he elected to walk in the screaming, bleeding man's direction. He rolled him over to find out where the blood was coming from, and made the alarming discovery that the man's eye had been ripped out, along with a huge chunk of flesh from his neck.

Grabbing Andre's arm, the man cried out for help.

Coming to his senses (finally!), Andre decided to run upstairs, as well. When he got outside, the police had arrived, as the family had phoned them.

And in a delightful plot twist, the family was so impressed with Andre's concern about the bleeding, shrieking man in the corner that they went ahead and bought the house from him.

Even though God only knows what happened there.

TAKEAWAY:

Even when there's blood, even when there's screaming,

even when the police are called and it's pretty clear someone was being tortured – You Do Not GIVE UP THE SALE!

CLOSING STRATEGY:
(1) Always give the clients all the information you can.
(2) Always race to the aid of an anguished prisoner with a missing eye.

♨ *Tyshea K.*
Wedding Specialist
Wedding Gowns
15 years in sales

I know we're all worn out after that last tale, but it's my job as a bringer of truth to now introduce you to another highly intense sector of the sales world. It's extremely colorful and pleasant on the surface, but at times it gets highly emotional...and even dangerous.

I'm referring, of course, to the <u>wedding gown</u> industry.

Tyshea K. got into wedding gown sales because she enjoys clothes and money, so here was a place where she could enjoy both at the same time. When asked if she has a closing strategy, she smiles and says, "The clothes speak for themselves."

Moreover, Tyshea measures success in the form of repeat customers and referrals. One time she even got a repeat visit from someone who never became her customer the first time around:

"I had a woman come in with her family to pick out a dress. She loved this one dress, but her family didn't, so they went elsewhere. Unfortunately, the other place messed up her dress, so the day of her wedding she came back to me to see if the dress was still available. It was, but needed to be hemmed and dyed. Needless to say, we put a super rush on the order and got it to her right before the wedding."

A lovely tale of saleswoman heroism, but as I've made clear, this particular business does have its dark side:

You see, early in Tyshea's career, she messed up a gown order. The color came back *slightly off!* (I know, I know...and I apologize for offending any of my readers.) The customer stormed out of the shop in tears. As for the customer's mother, she started screaming like Al Pacino on his worst acting day. The manager came out and yelled, "Calm down lady! *We're sorry the dress is pinkish-red instead of reddish-pink!"*

But the lady would not listen to reason. On and on she yelled, to the point where Tyshea approached her with a renewed apology. In return, Tyshea got her arm grabbed and found herself getting pushed down to the floor.

At which point the woman began to *kick* her.

Trying to intervene again, the manager attempted to stop the assault, but the woman pulled out a small knife! Thankfully, some other customers rushed in and restrained her.

She ran out before the police showed up, but eventually she got charged with assault and battery.

And you don't even want to KNOW about how things went when they ordered their cake!

TAKEAWAY:
In any business, the customers *care.* And oftentimes, they really, REALLY care.

CLOSING STRATEGY:

If you've got fine threads, you ain't got nothing to dread.

★ Phil D.
Account Executive
Raw Materials
7 years in sales

Okay, let's give the intensity a rest for (just) a moment.

Phil D.'s an electrician by trade, but he went into sales to boost his income. Judging from the annual condition of his W-2 (which is the tool he uses to measure success), Phil has done very well in that regard. When he hears whispers about salespeople being arrogant, he just brushes it off, because he knows in his heart that that's unfair.

For example, Phil once orchestrated a way to sell discounted building materials to his neighborhood church so they could build a community center in the "hood." Growing up, Phil had never had such a place at his disposal, so helping to create one for disadvantaged kids made him feel good about his job.

And if that doesn't persuade you that salespeople have heart, then check out this story of Phil's:

He went to a prospect's home to discuss a purchase order, only to learn that the guy wasn't there. His wife answered and said he'd be back later, so Phil thanked her and went on his way.

And then he heard a high-pitched scream.

The next thing Phil knew, the woman had opened the door again and was telling him her water had just

125

broke. "I'm all alone," she said. "Can you bring me to the hospital?"

So Phil D. did exactly that.

Only problem was, it was rush hour. The traffic was piled high in the sky. As the poor woman struggled to take in some breath, Phil started going the wrong way down one-way streets.

Eventually, the police took notice.

But they had sympathy, and gave him an escort to the hospital.

In the end, as it happened, the prospect didn't give Phil any business. But Phil got something even better, and it came to him by way of a letter in the mail.

The letter was addressed to Phil's CEO. The couple thanked Phil for his heroism on the day of their child's birth.

And they said that they'd named their child after him.

TAKEAWAY:
There's more to life, sometimes, than just the sale.

CLOSING STRATEGY:
Natural childbirth. (wink)

Raji S.
Sr. Sales Engineer
Turbine/Jet Engines
32 years in sales

When Raji S. worked as a waiter, he was lucky to get a 15-percent tip.

Selling turbine/jet engines proved to be a far more lucrative avenue to travel. He had studied Engineering and was intensely qualified when it came to presenting his expertise about his product.

His closing strategy is rather straightforward: Sell something that's in high demand and in short supply. When you get into such a market, there aren't many window shoppers there to waste your time.

In other words, when the phone rings, it's typically time to close rather than "open."

A selfless man by nature, Raji measures his success in accordance with his clients' success. If they have achieved their goals, then he has achieved his.

Although of course that measuring stick gets a little trickier when you're selling to a dictator...

Raji will never forget the time when he went into Iraq to sell a large order of jet engines to the government. The Iraqis didn't bore him with middlemen – they took him straight to the big cheese: Saddam Hussein.

Various military men sat with them. The setting was an outlandish castle.

The meeting was business as usual (save for the

famous clientele) until 10 beautiful women were led into the room. Raji was encouraged to let the ladies "take care of" him through his extended stay.

In some cases, negotiations of this kind could last for weeks on end. Therefore, Raji wasn't asked to select 1 of the 10; he was asked to select all 10!

He couldn't believe his discomfort. For one thing, he was married. For another thing, these women (ranging from 19 to 24 in age) could have been his own daughters!

On the other hand, rejecting the Iraqis' offer would have made them furious.

So Raji shacked up with the 10 women in his quarters. That way no one got in trouble. And rather than exploit them, he let them be in charge, and treated them like queens.

In the end, the oddness was more than worth it: Raji bagged an order for just north of a BILLION DOLLARS.

They purchased over 600 engines. Raji had not only impressed them with his engineering knowledge, he also had them enthralled with stateside information about American sports and movies.

TAKEAWAY:
Oftentimes the client will present cultural differences that call for delicate navigation. Once in a blue moon, the client will run a foreign nation with a history of military conflict with the United States (though I wouldn't lose sleep worrying about that one).

CLOSING STRATEGY:

Put the client's needs before your own. And the needs of the client's 10 women.

🖋 *Greg S.*
Account Manager
Pharmaceuticals
8 years in sales

Originally, Greg S. went to med school. The problem was, he didn't want to be a doctor. However, he really enjoyed being a hospital.

Since being a *patient* in the hospital isn't any fun, Greg decided to go into selling pharmaceuticals.

On the matter of closing, he wastes no time. He just pulls out the contract and asks for the business. Talk about an assertive bedside manner!

One time, however, it wasn't so easy. A doctor whom Greg was trying to close said to him, "I'll tell you what: I'll consider buying from you. But first you have to take my daughter out on a date."

If Greg honored this request, said the doctor, he'd find himself getting the largest order of his career.

"I don't understand," Greg protested, having no clue what this "daughter" character was all about. "Why ME?"

With a sparkle in his eye, the doctor said the two of them were a match made in heaven.

Long story short, Greg went on the date.

And bagged the huge order.

And went on to get engaged with the lovely lady.

TAKEAWAY:

Don't stop at asking for the deal or the money; always be sure to ask if there's a potential spouse in the mix.

CLOSING STRATEGY:

Pull out the contract. Ask for the business. Marry the doctor's daughter.

🦈 *A.J. S.*
Associate Sales Specialist
Food & Beverage
1.5 years in sales

When it comes to food and beverage sales, A.J. S. still has a lot to learn.

He's new to the trade, you see, so he's learning how to sell and how to close (and how to parse the difference between the two). When his boss "took the training wheels off" for the first time and let him run a full sale, A.J. was electrified. He cold called the prospect, explained the benefits and returns related to their service, and later dove in to make the presentation.

The sound of the client stating an intent to make a purchase was music to A.J.'s ears.

Indeed, I believe A.J. has a bright future in food and beverage sales, if only he simply learns a single (major) lesson:

You have to keep your own food and beverages down after you consume them!

You see, during A.J.'s first sale (described swiftly and vaguely, just above), he had to make a PowerPoint presentation. His nerves got the better of him, and his breakfast ended up all over the conference room floor.

Fortunately, nobody important was watching!

I mean, you know, the *Owners* were there. And the *Vice-President*. And a higher-ranked *Salesperson*. But, you know, it's not like the *President of the United States* was in the room...

After he puked, A.J. ran out into the hall. While standing there mortified, he saw an owner step outside and walk toward him. He tightened up with terror.

But the owner said everything would be okay.

And you know what else? Based on their sympathy for A.J.'s inexperience and vulnerability, the client went for the purchase.

TAKEAWAY:
Don't pretend you're superhuman. Sometimes vulnerability will break the ice.

CLOSING STRATEGY:
Hit pause on the PowerPoint and throw up all over the floor.

🖋 *Charlie B.*
Account Manager
Theater Rentals
33 years in sales

Tucked away in an old-fashioned playhouse off of Hollywood Boulevard in Los Angeles, Charlie shakes his head as he recalls the "good old days."

"Our whole culture's dying!" he declares, screaming at the top of his lungs as though he's in a... play of some kind.

"It used to be," he goes on, "that the people – the public! – wanted to see DRAMA! Now, we mostly rent this place out to aspiring actors who are putting on showcases."

Charlie then explains to me that "showcases" are performances in which an actor or actress – or a group of performers – stage little scenes and sections of well-known plays for the sake of showing agents and managers how good they are.

"Only most of the time they're not good," says Charlie, striking a match and lighting the tobacco in his wooden pipe. "It's pathetic, actually. No craft, just ego..."

Charlie wears a thick wool sweater, even though L.A. seems to be well in the middle of a lethal summer heatwave. He also – judging from his appearance – hasn't had a haircut in quite some time. After being around him for more than a couple of minutes, one cannot help but become filled with a feeling of dread.

"It's the end of the world," he says to me, a grave, fading sparkle in one of his eyes. "A world without literacy?!" he screams. "Where THEATER DOESN'T MATTER?!" he shouts.

Then he proceeds to break down and sob for a full ten minutes (I checked my watch).

Amidst all the talk of theater and drama, and all of Charlie's actual drama, it took me a while to get going with the sales questions. When I finally did, he looked at me as though I were mad.

"It sells itself," he said to me. "You want to make easy money? Sell to people who are desperate to become famous. There's always a lot of them, and they'll spare no expense to make it happen. Take out loans, call their mothers for help. I see it every day."

TAKEAWAY:

I feel like calling my mother. Not for financial help, but because apparently the world is ending!

CLOSING STRATEGY:

Position yourself in a market wherein the buyers are pursuing a life dream. Hollywood's got lots of them. You never catch a headshot photographer, acting reel editor, or theater rental salesperson standing around bored.

🖋 *Bernadette*
Sales Clerk
Used Books
18 years in sales

I met Bernadette the day after I met Charlie the theater rental guy, and to be honest I was expecting more grandiose speeches about the death of culture. After all, Bernadette not only sells books, but *used* books, which appeal to a very specific kind of buyer.

Refreshingly, I didn't find her to be hopeless or grave. I actually found Bernadette to be filled with enthusiasm for her job and the product she was selling.

"I love books," she said to me, "so it's great to be able to talk about them all day."

I quickly learned that in the used book trade, knowledge of the product is virtually everything. And I'm not talking about its price; I'm referring to actual substantive data on what's inside those books.

"Have you read all of them?" I asked her.

She half nodded, half shook her head, then smiled at me and said, "Most."

But devouring all the merchandise wasn't exactly the point. It was enough that Bernadette be well-versed in the various authors on her bookshelves, and – most critically – be able to make referrals.

"If somebody likes dark fiction, for example," she explains, "they might come in looking for titles by Chuck Palahniuk, the author of 'Fight Club.'

"So after they've got a bunch of his books under their arm, I tell them about Eric Bogosian, who writes a similar kind of fiction but is less well known for it. Then they're buying books by him, too."

In other words, Bernadette's particular sales job has a lot to do with being a member of a very specific *culture*. As I listened to her, I got the very strong feeling that the less organic you are to this culture, the less seriously your buyers will take you.

Meaning: You have to be *one of them.*

Same goes for a lot of trades. Whereas many salespeople sell universal items – such as cars, cell phones, and cable TV packages – that apply to most or all of us, other salespeople are in more specialized fields, such as Bernadette's.

Yet as good as she was, I'm a salesman, too. So the book we spent the most time talking about...was this one.

TAKEAWAY:
If you're selling within a distinctive world, then you have to be a card-carrying citizen of that world, or the buyers will quickly sniff you out and cry, "TOURIST!"

CLOSING STRATEGY:
Know the product. Not just the price points, but what it's actually made of, and why it actually matters.

🜚 *Jesse*
Salesman
Marijuana
1 year in (legal) sales

"Dude," Jesse says to me, "it's like a brave new world and sh-t."

I'll say. We're standing up high in the mountains of Colorado, where marijuana was recently legalized, and where, as a result, a brand new economy is springing up around it. On the ride over to meet with Jesse, I turned on the radio and heard that Denver actually had a round-the-clock *comedy* radio station!

Oh yeah, this was definitely a pot smoker's city.

When I started planning this book, I would have never dreamed of including a product such as Jesse's, but hey – if it's legal, it's legal. Jesse exists at the start of a brand new wave of commerce, at least in his state and a couple of others.

"What's the biggest change?" I ask him, knowing that in light of the new regulations and tax requirements, selling marijuana isn't as straightforward as it used to be. On the other hand, now you don't have to do it in dark corners, looking over your shoulders for the cops.

"It's just...all the official paperwork," he tells me. "Collecting a sales tax. Keeping invoices, that kind of stuff."

"Are the customers happy or sad that it's gone

legit?"

"Most everyone is happy," he tells me. "It's an exciting time. There are some people who gripe about our product possibly losing its edge now that it's legal, but alcohol never stopped being appealing, and that's been legal for almost a century now."

I figured Jesse exemplified the principle of having to be part of the culture you're selling to, but late in our encounter, he drops a bomb on me:

"I stopped smoking a few months ago."

My eyes pop out of my head. Given his long hair, tie-dye T-shirt, and glassy eyes, I had taken it for granted that he was "down with the cause."

"Nah," he says. "Used to be. Loooong time. And I'll miss it, but it gets old after a while. My lady and I are having a baby soon, so I don't really want it in my life at this point in time."

Staggering. Talk about irony: The moment the stuff becomes legal, a guy like Jesse – whom I'd call a "pothead" no matter what he puts in his body – casts it aside. I imagine there are always lots of surprises when something crosses from the black market to the legitimate market, and it'll certainly be fascinating to check back in on Denver in another ten years.

TAKEAWAY:
Commerce is as human as eating, drinking, and sleeping. If something is desirable to human beings, then there's a natural market it for it. Sometimes, however,

the sale will be illegal – though most of the time it will be legal. Then you have those times when the nature of a product's legality is in transition...

CLOSING STRATEGY:
Keep up with the times. It's a fast-moving world. What's red on Tuesday may be black by Thursday, so know your product's standing in the market and act accordingly.

Reginald
Sales rep
Sunglasses
4 years in sales

"Sunglasses are timeless," Reginald says to me. "They never go out of style – know why that is?"

I smile and shake my head.

"It's because they combine two things," he says. "Fashion and practicality. If it was only fashion, they would have been a passing fad. But as long as the sun is in the sky, people will have a need to keep it out of their eyes."

Jeez, and here I thought I was just chatting with some regular kid. Turns out Reginald was not only a sunglasses salesman, but some kind of holy-man-philosopher in disguise. And just when I thought the whole thing about "fashion and practicality" was his only theory, he kept on going:

"It also has a lot to do with darkness," he explains. "Darkness never goes out of style, neither. Again, it's just part of life: There's light, there's darkness. Ain't no getting around it. So when people put their sunglasses on, it's like they feel a bit of privacy, like they're in their own dark room..."

After turning my brain back around to a forward-facing position, I ask Reginald, "So is that what your customers want? Privacy?"

He laughs, giving me a wave of his hand. "Nah. I mean, maybe that's part of the deeper psychology.

But straight-up, it ain't consciously about what I'm discussing right now.

"In general, these folks just want to look cool.

"And that crosses all ages. I sell to teenagers, college kids, men in their sixties, and little kids holding their parents' hands. When people walk in here, it's almost like they go into a mode where they start acting a little tough. They don't realize it, but that's what sunglasses bring out of people. You want to fit in when you wear them. It's about looking somewhat mysterious, giving yourself mystique."

Even though I'd worn sunglasses many times in my life, never before had I stopped to realize any of the things he was saying...all of which happened to be true.

"And the other thing," he adds, "is it has to do with the eyes. See, the eyes are how you read a person. But the dude wearing sunglasses can't be read. So in a way, putting on sunglasses sends a social signal: *You can't access me so easily.*

"And that won't ever go out of style, either."

TAKEAWAY:
Whoa!

CLOSING STRATEGY:
It pays to be a genius. And all kidding aside: It pays to understand why your product appeals to people on a deep psychological level. Watch the customers' behavior. Get a sense of what they're truly after. Take

your product's appeal for granted, and you'll miss out on many opportunities to connect with a buyer and make a sale.

🐾 *Conner*

Sales
Vegetarian Hot Dogs
9 years in sales

Walking up to Conner's truck, I fully expect just a regular hot dog vendor. But when I take a close look at the menu, I have to be honest – I feel a little duped.

"Your truck says 'hot dogs,'" I say to him.

"Yes," Conner smiles, a deep blue sparkle in his eyes.

"But these aren't hot dogs."

"They may not be meat," he says, applying the patience of a man who's clearly had this conversation a zillion times before, "but you should taste one."

I look all around us. Many other food vendors are present at this flea market, selling hamburgers, pizza, dessert items, and even real hot dogs!

Then I look back at Conner. "Why should I choose you when I can get the real thing?"

"For starters," he explains, "it's healthy."

"You don't think 'hot dog' if you want to eat healthy. What else you got?"

His patience is completely unbreakable. "In addition," he says, "it'll give you a story to tell people. 'You know what I ate the other day? A vegan hot dog...'"

For a moment, that sounds completely ridiculous. For one thing, I have to stop and wonder why he's not using the other classic vegetarian pitches, such as, "It's good for the animals," or "It's good for the environment." For another thing, why in the world would I buy something just to "tell a story"?

Then – within a split-second – his logic starts to dawn on me. He can't use the classic pitches because they make the buyer feel guilt. Nobody wants to think about animal rights or the environment when they're just hungry! And as it happens, this whole "story to tell" angle isn't half bad. Sure, it sounds a little corny at first, but if you think about it, trying something new isn't only good for you personally – it also enables you to bond with new kinds of people.

And everybody has a use for that.

So I buy the hot dog. And it wasn't half bad! I'm not about to stop by that truck every day, but I gotta admit the guy did something that's not particularly easy:

He sold me.

TAKEAWAY:
Beneath every product is an experience. So when you're buying the physical thing, you're also buying something deeper, which you'll remember.

CLOSING STRATEGY:
If you're selling something that appeals to a minority segment of the population, don't try to appeal to the majority with aggression or loud messaging. Slip in from the side, appealing to traits of theirs that are more fun and relatable.

PART III:
"ACT AS IF": DRESSING FOR SUCCESS

"The apparel oft proclaims the man"
~ William Shakespeare

Now, if you're a salesperson who's able to hide behind a telephone or a computer, I don't have any clothing advice for you. Dress however you want. If you're using a phone, you'll need to focus on your voice (more on that in a moment). If you're communicating with clients via email or another form of web communication, you'll need to focus on your English (more on that, too, in just a moment).

But as for what you wear in those cases, you can dress up like the Easter Bunny for all I care.

However, most of you will not be concealed to the prospect or client's eye. Most of you, in fact, will be in plain sight...and be that as it may, let's hope you're not a plain sight.

In sales, there's an old expression that goes "Act as if." It basically means to carry yourself in the most impressive way possible to make yourself part of the sales presentation. Accordingly, act as if you're the best salesperson in the world. Act as if you drove a Ferrari to the meeting. Act as if your wife's the foxiest lady on the block.

If you saw that flick BOILER ROOM, you know they've got a great routine in there about the "Act as if" concept (and it's a couple degrees more profane than mine above). Just remember: The client's not psychic. The client can't see your vulnerabilities or fears. For all the client knows, you sell a million bucks worth of merchandise a month.

So act that way.

Now, as you know by way of the heading above, part of acting as if is Dressing The Part. You can't blow 'em away without the right clothing. This doesn't mean you have to spend 90 percent of your salary on incredibly expensive clothes; in fact, the cost isn't really a key issue here.

What's important is that YOU play to YOUR strengths and look your BEST.

Now what does that mean, exactly?

COLOR

What colors look good on you? Women are better at this stuff than guys, but no matter what your sex is, if you don't know what your best colors are, then ask somebody you trust. Spouse, best friend, even a clothing store worker.

Sometimes the right amount of green can light up your eyes, making you look way smarter than you have any right to (no offense!).

Sometimes darker shades are just the thing, making you look intense, filled with depth, and worth taking seriously.

You alone will be able to figure out what colors enhance your physical presence the most. And this isn't only about looks; it's also about practically. For example, don't show up to a meeting at an Italian restaurant dressed in white; you'll end up with visible spaghetti sauce all over your clothes! And do me a favor and avoid the orange checkered suit if you've been hired to sell funeral caskets. Believe me, even if orange checkers look dynamite on you, it's gonna backfire.

CLASS

What class level should you aim for?

This is half determined by you, and half determined by the product.

Let's look at you first. If you're a raw type who excels when being down-to-Earth and plainspoken, don't show up wearing a fancy suit. The whole tone will be wrong. It'll seem like you're trying too hard. Just go for business casual, or even straight-up casual, and play directly to your own strengths as a seller. On the flip-side, maybe you grew up in an affluent community and have the gaze, speech patterns, and mannerisms of an upscale cat. Great! Then play right to that: Dress to the nines, splash on some cologne or perfume, and blow 'em away by exuding luxury.

Again, as with color, you alone know what will work. Start by examining your strengths as a salesperson and build from there. If you're known for being funny, go more casual. Known for being intelligent, go more formal. Look great with a five o'clock shadow? Avoid the GQ suit and stick with the button-up shirt with no tie.

Now, as I said, a huge part of the class-level pie chart is what you're selling. Chances are, the people who hired you have already been matchmakers in terms of pairing you with your product or service. In other words, it's very likely you already fit what you're selling. At used car dealerships, you tend to encounter more blue collar attitudes then you do at upscale car dealerships. At retail outlets, you run into teenagers and college kids. In general, whatever's being sold is a tonal fit for the seller.

That said, you should still make sure the fit is nice and tight. If you're selling something that's appealing on account of its reasonable pricing, an expensive suit can really backfire. On the other hand, dressing down to sell a luxury item might not only send a mixed message, but annoy or offend the sensibilities of the upscale client.

Think it over. Pick the level. And pay attention to the prospects' and clients' eyes when they give you that first once-over. If you've selected wisely, their eyes will show unquestionable respect.

HIERARCHY

Here's an important one that slips some people's minds:

Whatever you wear, and as wise and thoughtful as your selections are, be careful to be mindful of what your coworkers have on. Because although standing out amongst clients and prospects is a terrific thing, standing out too much back at the office can blow up in your face. People will get envious and competitive. They'll whisper about you, wondering who you think you are. Now, depending on where you work, the gang might be good-humored or friendly enough for the previous sentences to sound silly. If that's the case, then do your thing – and go team!

But whatever your personal situation, be sure to be conscious of your surroundings. For one thing, don't outshine your superiors. If they see you're better dressed than they are, they'll think you're after their jobs. Maybe you are, but don't draw that much attention to it! As for your equals, it's one thing to dress a notch or two above them; that won't create any waves. But if the whole office goes for business casual and you decide to wear suits, just know that you're creating a potential controversy.

The key word here is "politics," and for worse or for better, politics are as important to your job longevity as actual selling skills. So be alert. Don't outshine your superiors, and if you outshine your peers, do so in a way that's grounded and not flamboyant.

Because no salesperson succeeds all alone. We need supportive teammates who don't feel like we're trying to one-up them. Healthy competition is great; grandstanding tends to be negative in the end.

A NOTE FOR THE TELEPHONE SALESPERSON

If you're working on the phone, you can still "Act as if," but in this case your voice and your mind are your key weapons. Your voice has to sound good and pleasing to the ear. No matter what your particular accent may be, this can be achieved. Speak calmly. Speak gently, even. Allow the prospect or client's audio environment to be a pleasant one. Don't take this so far as to put them to sleep, but take control of the sound environment in as subtle and penetrating a way as possible.

Doing this calls for a degree of "matching," too. If you've got a fast talker on the line, go faster. A slow talker? Slow it down already! Someone who's older may need you to be louder, and someone who's younger may need you to get to the point already. So feel it out: Who have you got on the other end? Shape your voice accordingly.

As for your mind, its strengths are your strengths as a salesperson. If you think fast, then dazzle them with your ability to rapidly unload critical information. If you have excellent attention to detail, then make the clients swoon with beautiful feats of description. Naturally, these ethics apply whether or not you're on the phone, but when there's no physical presence to concentrate on, the quality of your thinking will be center stage.

A NOTE FOR THE ONLINE SALESPERSON

If you're using email or communicating online in some other way, be sure to muscle up on your spelling and grammar. All of us are human, and that means we're capable of typos and misspelled words, and that's okay with our friends and loved ones. But in a professional context, even someone who's intelligent in every measurable way will get branded with one word due to sloppy writing:

MORON!

So act as if. Act as if you're William Shakespeare. Okay, that's probably going too far. Crazed flights of poetry will probably be too alienating (unless you're selling at a classic bookstore or something). But act as if you OWN the English language. Tighten up those sentences. Get to the point. Proofread; don't hit Send until you've cleared that message of any bugs.

On a deep level, the person on the other end will register your communication care as indicative of overall care and professionalism.

In summary, no matter where you are, what you're selling, or what you've got to work with...ACT AS IF.

☕ CONCLUSION

It's been quite a ride, and I'm honored that you've shown up to take it with me.

We've studied salespeople from a ton of angles. We've seen them from their own points-of-view, from the viewpoints of others, through the prisms of their unique stories and memories, and through the lens of pop culture. We've come to understand the things that make them different from one another and different from the world at large – yet just the same as everyone else.

Hopefully, now that we've reached the end, we've weakened some of the stereotypes that exist about salespeople, and replaced them with newer, more positive alternatives. And if that hasn't been your particular experience, then (A) shame on you!, and (B) I have faith that society will continue to understand us better as time goes on.

Before I leave you to your coffee, I'd like to share just one last story – one which I feel captures the unique soul of salespeople unlike any other (including DEATH OF A SALESMAN!):

There was once a man living in Boston, Massachusetts – an immigrant in the middle of the 20th century. His family – a wife and three sons – was located back in Europe, but he had sailed across the Atlantic Ocean to pursue the American Dream, and make enough money to move the four of them to the United States, as well.

The problem was, America was not quite as he'd expected it to be. Indeed, it had a stronger economy than he had ever seen before in his life. The people in America enjoyed large portions of food and living in spacious, comfortable homes. Although many of them were poor, there were plenty of resources, and the prevailing sense that one could achieve great wealth and happiness if one was simply willing to work hard enough.

The immigrant was certainly willing to work. So he began to spend his mornings walking along the city streets, offering to help out the businesses near his apartment in any way he could. The results were generally frustrating to him.

The doctor's office didn't need help, as the immigrant lacked sufficient training to be able to assist them in a meaningful way.

The same went for the law office: They didn't need a man with imperfect English and no knowledge of American law to aid them in their daily activities.

The tailoring shop had a similar complaint. So did the baker, and the barber, and even the dog groomer.

In fact, although some of the businesses were willing to be helpful, the only help they offered was a position wherein the immigrant could sweep the floor.

Out of pride, he refused to do such a thing. Reason being, he not only knew he was overqualified for such a job, but he knew that a janitorial position would not be a good option to get his family moved over from Europe.

One night, feeling short on luck, the immigrant

went to a bar and had a drink. The bartender got him to open up and discuss his problems. "You're a nice, charming guy," said the bartender, trying to cheer him up. "You can't have any problem that's too awful..."

Smiling a bit, the immigrant summed it all up, and capped off his story by saying, "The problem with me is, it seems like my kindness and charm is all I've got. If only there was a job where I got a chance to chat with people, and got rewarded for treating them well."

The bartender wore a knowing smile. The immigrant didn't see what was worth smiling about. Leaning across the bar, the bartender said, "You've just identified your gift."

"What's that?"

"You're a natural born salesman."

And so he was. The next day, he went back to the tailor's shop, and said that although he couldn't sew any suits, he certainly would be able to help sell a bunch.

Nodding, the tailor said, "That's not a bad idea. I can't stand dealing with the customers. I just like doing the tailoring."

Our friend the immigrant patted the tailor's shoulder. He said to him, "Not to worry. I love people. And I'll be pleased to deal with your customers."

He went on to have tremendous success, and his family was able to join him within four short months.

Dear reader, I wish you the very same success as the man in that tale. Whether you're selling, or being sold, it doesn't matter. The bottom line is that you're a person. And person or salesperson, you deserve, and should demand maximum happiness. Now go close something and enjoy a cup of coffee!!!

GLOSSARY

Rainmakers – These are the sales people that "make it rain". They consistently exceed their quotas, and make ton of money.

Rock Stars – top of the food chain sales people, creme de la creme. See "A-Players"

Discovery calls – Introductory calls with prospects. These are used to get an understanding of their wants and needs.

POC – Proof of capabilities. This is where you prove the capabilities of your services or products.

Quota – The total dollar figure that a salesperson is responsible for during a given timeframe. The majority of quotas are either monthly or quarterly, but a few organizations distribute them annually.

Pipeline/Sales Funnel – This is the number, and total dollar figure of opportunities that one has qualified as a viable sales target.

10x – This could be 5x, 2x, 20x, etc. Typically this is used as a multiplier of your total quota versus your opportunity. Ex. Your quota is $100k and you have $1million in opportunities, this is equal to 10x your pipeline.

Presidents Club/Winners Circle - There are various names for this "club", but essentially this is the top 10-20% of sales people within a company. Most companies offer awards, money/bonuses, and even annual trips for the individuals that achieve this prestigious milestone.

Corporate Athlete - Most salespeople are competitive and come from team/competitive environments, so it is most fitting to consider your top tier salespeople this.

AM - Account Manager

AE – Account Executive

SAE – Senior Account Executive

SD - Sales Director/Director of Sales

CSO – Chief Sales Officer

Leads – Can be names of companies, and/or contact information of companies that could potentially benefit from the product or services that a salesperson offers.

ROI - Return On Investment. Typically this is what most buyers are interested in depending on the products/services you are selling.